THE CRISIS

Titles on History in Prometheus's Great Minds Series

See the back of this volume for a complete list of titles in Prometheus's Great Books in Philosophy and Great Minds series.

THE CRISIS

THOMAS
PAINE

GREAT MINDS SERIES

 Prometheus Books

59 John Glenn Drive
Amherst, New York 14228-2119

Published 2008 by Prometheus Books

Inquiries should be addressed to
Prometheus Books
59 John Glenn Drive
Amherst, New York 14228–2119

716–691–0133 (x210). FAX: 716–691–0137.
WWW.PROMETHEUSBOOKS.COM

12 11 10 09 08   5 4 3 2 1

Library of Congress Cataloging-in-Publication Data

Paine, Thomas, 1737–1809.
    The crisis / by Thomas Paine.
        p. cm.
    Originally published: New York : Peter Eckler Pub. Co., 1918.
    ISBN 978-1-59102-631-0 (pbk.)
    1. United States—History—Revolution, 1775–1783. 2. United
States—History—Revolution, 1775–1783—Causes. 3 United States—Politics and government—1775–1783. 4. Great Britain—Politics and government—1760–1780. 5. Political science—Early works to 1800. I Title.

E211.P1193 2008
973.3—dc22   2008027888

Printed in the United States of America on acid-free paper

THOMAS PAINE was born in Thetford, England, on January 29, 1737. Forced to leave school early to enter his father's trade of corset making, he was never satisfied with this work. After attempting several other professions—including privateer, office worker, servant, and schoolteacher—with little success, he made acquaintance with Benjamin Franklin. Franklin persuaded Paine to leave England for the American colonies, and he arrived in Philadelphia in November 1774 with Franklin's letters of recommendation in hand. Paine found work as managing editor of the *Pennsylvania Magazine*, to which he contributed various poems and essays.

During this time of growing dissent within the colonies, Paine first called for reconciliation with England. However, after the battles of Lexington and Concord in 1775, he became an adamant propagandist for separation. In January 1776 he published his pamphlet *Common Sense*. This seminal work, which was first published anonymously, and his second insurrectionary pamphlet, *The Crisis*, exercised profound influence on public opinion and morale.

Following the War for Independence, Paine returned to England. He was initially welcomed as a celebrity, but the accolades soon ceased with the publication of *Rights of Man* (1791), a defense of the French Revolution meant to be a reply to Edmund Burke's *Reflections on the Revolution in France*. Forced to leave England because of the public outcry his book had provoked, Paine traveled to France, where he was granted citizenship. However, after he spoke out in defense of deposed king Louis XVI, Paine was imprisoned in 1793 for almost a year and nearly executed by the revolutionary government. While in prison, Paine began composing his statement of religious belief, *The Age of Reason*. Although pilloried as a declaration of atheism, *The Age of Reason* actually espoused deism—Paine rejected the inerrancy of the Bible and disputed revelation. He argued for a god who had created the universe and given humankind the gift of reason, which it would apply to the management of its own affairs and toward the discovery of the physical universe.

Paine returned to the United States in 1802. Though President Thomas Jefferson welcomed him, the former champion of liberty was ostracized by many as "that outrageous blasphemer." Thomas Paine died in New York City on June 8, 1809, all but forgotten. His obituary notice from the *New York Citizen* read in part: "He had lived long, did some good and much harm."

Nevertheless, the influence of *The Age of Reason* began to grow as the nineteenth century progressed and free thought challenged outdated religious beliefs. *Common Sense* and *The Crisis* remain as important works of literature in American history, and Thomas Paine is revered today for his great influence on the American Revolution, the French Revolution, and working-class reform in the United Kingdom.

THE CRISIS
NUMBER I

THESE are the times that try men's souls. The summer soldier and the sunshine patriot will, in this crisis, shrink from the service of his country; but he that stands it now, deserves the love and thanks of man and woman. Tyranny, like hell, is not easily conquered; yet we have this consolation with us, that the harder the conflict, the more glorious the triumph. What we obtain too cheap, we esteem too lightly: 'tis dearness only that gives every thing its value. Heaven knows how to put a proper price upon its goods; and it would be strange indeed, if so celestial an article as freedom should not be highly rated. Britain, with an army to enforce her tyranny, has declared that she has a right (not only to tax) but "to bind us in all cases whatsoever," and if being bound in that manner, is not slavery, then is there not such a thing as slavery upon earth. Even the expression is impious, for so unlimited a power can belong only to God.

Whether the independence of the continent was declared too soon, or delayed too long, I will not now enter into as an argument; my own simple opinion is, that had it been eight months earlier, it would have been much better. We did not make a proper use of last winter, neither could we, while we were in a dependant state. However, the fault, if it were one, was all our own; we have none to blame but ourselves. But no great deal is lost yet; all that Howe has been doing for this month past, is rather a ravage than a conquest, which the spirit of the Jerseys a year ago would have quickly repulsed, and which time and a little resolution will soon recover.

I have as little superstition in me as any man living, but my secret opinion has ever been, and still is, that God Almighty will not give up a people to military destruction, or leave them unsupportedly to perish, who have so earnestly and so repeatedly sought to avoid the calamities of war, by every decent method which wisdom could invent. Neither have I so much of the infidel in me, as to suppose that He has relinquished the government of the world, and given us up to the care of devils; and as I do not, I cannot see on what grounds the king of Britain can look up to heaven for help against us: a common murderer, a highwayman, or a house-breaker, has as good a pretence as he.

'Tis surprising to see how rapidly a panic will sometimes run through a country. All nations and ages have been subject to them: Britain has trembled like an ague at the report of a French fleet of flat bottomed boats; and in the fourteenth century the whole English army, after ravaging the kingdom of France, was driven back like men petrified with fear; and this brave exploit was performed by a few broken forces collected and headed by a woman, Joan of Arc. Would that heaven might inspire some Jersey maid to spirit up her countrymen, and save her fair fellow sufferers from ravage and ravishment! Yet panics, in some cases, have their uses; they produce as much good as hurt. Their duration is always short; the mind soon grows through them, and acquires a firmer habit than before. But their peculiar advantage is, that they are the touchstones of sincerity and hypocrisy, and bring things and men to light, which might otherwise have lain forever undiscovered. In fact, they have the same effect on secret traitors, which an imaginary apparition would have upon a private murderer. They sift out the hidden thoughts of man, and hold them up in public to the world. Many a disguised tory has lately shown his head, that shall penitentially solemnize with curses the day on which Howe arrived upon the Delaware.

As I was with the troops at Fort Lee, and marched with them to the edge of Pennsylvania, I am well acquainted with many circumstances, which those who live at a distance, know but little or nothing of. Our situation there was exceedingly cramped, the place being a narrow neck of land between the North River and the Hackensack. Our force was inconsiderable, being not one-fourth so great as Howe could bring against us. We had no army at hand to have relieved the garrison, had we shut ourselves up and stood on the defence. Our ammunition, light artillery, and the best part of our stores, had been removed, on the apprehension that Howe would endeavor to penetrate the Jerseys, in which case Fort Lee could be of no use to us; for it must occur to every thinking man, whether in the army or not, that these kind of field forts are only for temporary purposes, and last in use no longer than the enemy directs his force against the particular object, which such forts are raised to defend. Such was our situation and condition at Fort Lee on the morning of the 20th of November, when an officer arrived with information that the enemy with two hundred boats had landed about seven or eight miles above: Major General Green, who commanded the garrison, immediately ordered them under arms, and sent express to his excellency, General Washington, at the town of Hackensack, distant by the way of the ferry, six miles. Our first object was to secure the bridge over the Hackensack, which laid up the river between the enemy and us, about six miles from us, and three miles from them. General Washington arrived in about three-quarters of an hour, and marched at the head of the troops towards the bridge, which place I expected we should have a brush for; however, they did not choose to dispute it with us, and the greatest part of our troops went over the bridge, the rest over the ferry, except some which passed at a mill on a small creek, between the bridge and. the ferry, and made their way through some marshy grounds up to the town of Hackensack, and there passed the river. We brought off as much baggage as the wagons could contain, the rest was lost. The simple object was to bring off the garrison, and to march them on till theycould be strengthened by the Jersey or Pennsylvania militia, so as to be enabled to make a stand. We staid four days at Newark, collected in our out-posts with some Jersey militia, and marched out twice to meet the enemy, on being informed that they were advancing, though our numbers were greatly inferior to theirs. Howe, in my little opinion, committed a great error in generalship in not throwing a body of forces off from Staten Island through Amboy, by which means he might have seized all our stores at Brunswick, and intercepted our march into Pennsylvania: but if we believe the power of hell to be limited, we must likewise believe that their agents are under some providential control.

I shall not now attempt to give all the particulars of our retreat to the Delaware; suffice it for the present to say, that both officers and men, though greatly harrassed and fatigued, frequently without rest, covering, or provision, the inevitable consequences of a long retreat, bore it with a manly and mar-tial spirit. All their wishes centered in one, which was, that the country would turn out and help them to drive the enemy back. Voltaire has remarked that King William never appeared to full advantage but in difficulties and in action; the same remark may be made on General Washington, for the character fits him. There is a natural firmness in some minds which cannot be unlocked by trifles, but which, when unlocked, discovers a cabinet of fortitude; and I reckon it among those kind of public blessings, which we do not immediately see, that God hath blest him with uninterrupted health, and given him a mind that can even flourish upon care.

I shall conclude this paper with some miscellaneous remarks on the state of our affairs; and shall begin with asking the following question: Why is it that the enemy have left the New England provinces, and made these middle ones the seat of war? The answer is easy: New England is not infested with tories, and we are. I have been tender in raising the cry against these men, and, used numberless arguments to show them their danger, but it will not do to sacrifice a world to either their folly or their baseness. The period is now arrived, in which either they or we must change our sentiments, or one or both must fall. And what is a tory? Good God! what is he? I should not be afraid to go with a hundred whigs against a thousand tories, were they to attempt to get into arms. Every tory is a coward; for servile, slavish, self-interested fear is the foundation of toryism; and a man under such influence, though he may be cruel, never can be brave.

But, before the line of irrecoverable separation be drawn between us, let us reason the matter together: your conduct is an invitation to the enemy, yet not one in a thousand of you has heart enough to join him. Howe is as much deceived by you as the American cause is injured by you. He expects you will all take up arms, and flock to his standard, with muskets on your shoulders. Your opinions are of no use to him, unless you support him personally, for 'tis soldiers, and not tories, that he wants.

I once felt all that kind of anger, which a man ought to feel, against the mean principles that are held by the tories: a noted

one, who kept a tavern at Amboy, was standing at his door,
with as pretty a child in his hand, about eight or nine years old,
as I ever saw, and after speaking his mind as freely as he
thought was prudent, finished with this unfatherly expression,
"*Well! give me peace in my day.*" Not a man lives on the continent but fully believes that a separation must some time or
other finally take place, and a generous parent should have
said, "*If there must be trouble, let it be in my day, that my child
may have peace;*" and this single reflection, well applied, is
sufficient to awaken every man to duty. Not a place upon earth
might be so happy as America. Her situation is remote from all
the wangling world, and she has nothing to do but to trade with
them. A man can easily distinguish in himself between temper
and principle, and I am as confident, as I am that God governs
the world, that America will never be happy till she gets clear
of foreign dominion. Wars, without ceasing, will break out till
that period arrives, and the continent must in the end be conqueror; for though the flame of liberty may sometimes cease to
shine, the coal can never expire.

America did not, nor does not want force; but she wanted
a proper application of that force. Wisdom is not the purchase
of a day, and it is no wonder that we should err at the first setting off. From an excess of tenderness, we were unwilling to
raise an army, and trusted our cause to the temporary defence
of a well-meaning militia. A summer's experience has now
taught us better; yet with those troops, while they were collected, we were able to set bounds to the progress of the
enemy, and, thank God! they are again assembling. I always
considered militia as the best troops in the world for a sudden
exertion, but they will not do for a long campaign. Howe, it is
probable, will make an attempt on this city; should he fail on
this side the Delaware, he is ruined: if he succeeds, our cause

is no ruined. He stakes all on his side against a part on ours; admitting he succeeds, the consequence will be, that armies from both ends of the continent will march to assist their suffering friends in the middle states; for he cannot go every where; it is impossible. I consider Howe as the greatest enemy the tories have; he is bringing a war into their country, which, had it not been for him and partly for themselves, they had been clear of. Should he now be expelled, I wish with all the devotion of a Christian, that the names of whig and tory may never more be mentioned; but should the tories give him encouragement to come, or assistance if he come, I as sincerely wish that our next year's arms may expel them from the continent, and the congress appropriate their possessions to the relief of those who have suffered in well-doing. A single successful battle next year, will settle the whole. America could carry on a two years war by the confiscation of the property of disaffected persons, and be made happy by their expulsion. Say not that this is revenge, call it rather the soft resentment of a suffering people, who, having no object in view but the *good of all*, have staked their *own all* upon a seemingly doubtful event. Yet it is folly to argue against determined hardness; eloquence may strike the ear, and the language of sorrow draw forth the tear of compassion, but nothing can reach the heart that is steeled with prejudice.

Quitting this class of men, I turn with the warm ardor of a friend to those who have nobly stood, and are yet determined to stand the matter out: I call not upon a few, but upon all: not on *this* state or *that* state, but on *every* state; up and help us; lay your shoulders to the wheel; better have too much force than too little, when so great an object is at stake. Let it be told to the future world, that in the depth of winter, when nothing but hope and virtue could survive, that the city and the country, alarmed at one common danger, came forth to meet and to repulse it. Say not that thousands are gone, turn out your tens of thousands; throw not the burden of the day upon Providence, but "*show your faith by your works*," that God may bless you. It matters not where you live, or what rank of life you hold, the evil or the blessing will reach you all. The far and the near, the home counties and the back, the rich and the poor, will suffer or rejoice alike. The heart that feels not now, is dead: the blood of his children will curse his cowardice, who shrinks back at a time when a little might have saved the whole, and made *them* happy. I love the man that can smile in trouble, that can gather strength from distress, and grow brave by reflection. 'Tis the business of little minds to shrink; but he whose heart is firm, and whose conscience approves his conduct, will pursue his principles unto death. My own line of reasoning is to myself as straight and clear as a ray of light. Not all the treasures of the world, so far as I believe, could have induced me to support an offensive war, for I think it murder; but if a thief breaks into my house, burns and destroys my property, and kills or threatens to kill me, or those that are in it, and to "*bind me in all cases whatsoever*," to his absolute will, am I to suffer it? What signifies it to me, whether he who does it is a king or a common man; my countryman or not my countryman: whether it be done by an individual villain, or an army of them? If we reason to the root of things we shall find no difference; neither can any just cause be assigned why we should punish in the one case and pardon in the other. Let them call me rebel, and welcome, I feel no concern from it; but I should suffer the misery of devils, were I to make a whore of my soul by swearing allegiance to one whose character is that of a sottish, stupid, stubborn, worthless, brutish man. I conceive likewise a horrid idea in receiving mercy from a being, who at the last day shall be shrieking to the rocks and mountains to cover him, and fleeing with terror from the orphan, the widow, and the slain of America.

There are cases which cannot be overdone by language, and this is one. There are persons too who see not the full extent of the evil which threatens them, they solace themselves with hopes that the enemy, if they succeed, will be merciful. It is the madness of folly, to expect mercy from those who have refused to do justice; and even mercy, where conquest is the object, is only a trick of war; the cunning of the fox is as murderous as the violence of the wolf; and we ought to guard equally against both. Howe's first object is partly by threats and partly by promises, to terrify or seduce the people to deliver up their arms and receive mercy. The ministry recommended the same plan to Gage, and this is what the tories call making their peace, *"a peace which passeth all understanding" indeed!* A peace which would be the immediate forerunner of a worse ruin than any we have yet thought of. Ye men of Pennsylvania, do reason upon these things! Were the back counties to give up their arms, they would fall an easy prey to the Indians, who are all armed: this perhaps is what some tories would not be sorry for. Were the home counties to deliever up their arms, they would be exposed to the resentment of the back counties, who would then have it in their power to chastise their defection at pleasure. And were any one state to give up its arms, *that* state must be garrisoned by all Howe's army of Britons and Hessians to preserve it from the anger of the rest. Mutual fear is the principal link in the chain of mutual love, and woe be to that state that breaks the compact. Howe is mercifully inviting you to barbarous destruction, and men must be either rogues or fools that will not see it.

I dwell not upon the powers of imagination; I bring reason to your ears; and in language as plain as A, B, C, hold up truth to your eyes.

I thank God that I fear not. I see no real cause for fear. I know our situation well, and can see the way out of it. While our army was collected, Howe dared not risk a battle, and it is no credit to him that he decamped from the White Plains, and waited a mean opportunity to ravage the defenceless Jerseys; but it is great credit to us, that, with a handful of men, we sustained an orderly retreat for near an hundred miles, brought off our ammunition, all our field pieces, the greatest part of our stores, and had four rivers to pass. None can say that our retreat was precipitate, for we were near three weeks in performing it, that the country might have time to come in. Twice we marched back to meet the enemy, and remained out till dark. The sign of fear was not seen in our camp, and had not some of the cowardly and disaffected inhabitants spread false alarms through the country, the Jerseys had never been ravaged. Once more we are again collected and collecting, our new army at both ends of the continent is recruiting fast, and we shall be able to open the next campaign with sixty thousand men, well armed and clothed. This is our situation, and who will may know it. By perseverance and fortitude we have the prospect of a glorious issue; by cowardice and submission, the sad choice of a variety of evils—a ravaged country a depopulated city— habitations without safety, and slavery without hope—our homes turned into barracks and bawdy-houses for Hessians, and a future race to provide for, whose fathers we shall doubt of. Look on this picture and weep over it! and if there yet remains one thoughtless wretch who believes it not, let him suffer it unlamented.

COMMON SENSE.
December 23, 1776.

THE CRISIS NUMBER II

To Lord Howe

What's in the name of lord *that I should fear*
To bring my grievance to the public ear?
—Churchill

UNIVERSAL empire is the prerogative of a writer. His concerns are with all mankind, and though he cannot command their obedience, he can assign them their duty. The Republic of Letters is more ancient than monarchy, and of far higher character in the world than the vassal court of Britain; he that rebels against reason is a real rebel, but he that in defence of reason, rebels against tyranny, has a better title to "*Defender of the Faith*," than George the third.

As a military man your lordship may hold out the sword of war, and call it the "*ultima ratio regum:*" *the last reason of Kings*; we in return can show you the sword of justice, and call it, "the best scourge of tyrants." The first of these two may threaten, or even frighten for a while, and cast a sickly langor over an insulted people, but reason will soon recover the debauch, and restore them again to tranquil fortitude. Your lordship, I find, has now commenced author, and published a *Proclamation*: I have published a *Crisis*; as they stand, they are the antipodes of each other; both cannot rise at once, and one of them must descend; and so quick is the revolution of things, that your lordship's performance, I see, has already fallen many degrees from its first place, and is now just visible on the edge of the political horizon.

It is surprising to what a pitch of infatuation, blind folly and obstinacy will carry mankind, and your lordship's drowsy proclamation is a proof that it does not even quit them in their sleep. Perhaps you thought America too was taking a nap, and therefore chose, like Satan to Eve, to whisper the delusion softly, lest you should awaken her. This continent sir, is too extensive to sleep all at once, and too watchful, even in its slumbers, not to startle at the unhallowed foot of an invader. You may issue your proclamations, and welcome, for we have learned to "reverence ourselves," and scorn the insulting ruffian that employs you. America, for your deceased brother's sake, would gladly have shown you respect, and it is a new aggravation to her feelings, that Howe should be forgetful, and raise his sword against those, who at their own charge raised a monument to his brother. But your master has commanded, and you have not enough of nature left to refuse. Surely! there must be something strangely degenerating in the love of monarchy, that can so completely wear a man down to an ingrate, and make him proud to lick the dust that kings have trod upon. A few more years, should you survive them, will bestow on you the title of "an old man": and in some hour of future reflection you may probably find the fitness of Wolsey's despairing penitence—"had I served my God as faithfully as I have served my king, he would not thus have forsaken me in my old age."

The character you appear to us in is truly ridiculous. Your friends, the tories, announced your coming, with high descriptions of your unlimited powers; but your proclamation has given them the lie, by showing you to be a commissioner without authority. Had your powers been ever so great, they were nothing to us, further than we pleased; because we had the same right which other nations had, to do what we thought was best. "*The* UNITED STATES of AMERICA," will sound as pompously in the world or in history, as "the Kingdom of Great Britain"; the character of *General Washington* will fill a page with as much lustre as that of *Lord Howe*: and the *congress* have as much right to command the *king and parliament* in London to desist from legislation, as *they* or *you* have to command the congress. Only suppose how laughable such an edict would appear from us, and then, in that merry mood, do but turn the tables upon yourself; and you will see how your proclamation is received here. Having thus placed you in a proper position in which you may have a full view of your folly, and learn to despise it, I hold up to you, for that purpose, the following quotation from your own lunarian proclamation. —"And we (Lord Howe and General Howe) do command (and in his majesty's name forsooth) all such persons as are assembled together, under the name of general, or provincial congresses, committees, conventions or other associations, by whatever name or names known and distinguished, to desist and cease from all such treasonable actings and doings."

You introduce your proclamation by referring to your declarations of the 14th of July and 19th of September. In the last of these, you sunk yourself below the character of a private gentleman. That I may not seem to accuse you unjustly, I shall state the circumstance: by a verbal invitation of yours, communicated to congress by General Sullivan, then a prisoner on his parole, you signified your desire of conferring with some members of that body as private gentlemen. It was beneath the dignity of the American congress to pay any regard to a message that at best was but a genteel affront, and had too much of the ministerial complexion of tampering with private persons; and which might probably have been the case, had the gentlemen who were deputed on the business, possessed that kind

of easy virtue which an English courtier is so truly distinguished by. Your request, however, was complied with, for
honest men are naturally more tender of their civil than their
political fame. The interview ended as every sensible man
thought it would; for your lordship knows, as well as the writer
of the *Crisis*, that it is impossible for the king of England to
promise the repeal, or even the revisal of any acts of parliament; wherefore, on your part, you had nothing to say, more
than to request, in the room of demanding, the entire surrender
of the continent; and then, if that was complied with, to
promise that the inhabitants should escape with their lives.
This was the upshot of the conference. You informed the con-
ferees that you were two months in soliciting these powers. We
ask, what powers? for as commissioner you have none. If you
mean the power of pardoning, it is an oblique proof that your
master was determined to sacrifice all before him; and that you
were two months in dissuading him from his purpose. Another
evidence of his savage obstinacy! From your own account of
the matter we may justly draw these two conclusions: 1st, That
you serve a monster; and 2d, That never was a messenger sent
on a more foolish errand than yourself. This plain language
may perhaps sound uncouthly to an ear vitiated by courtly
refinements; but words were made for use, and the fault lies in
deserving them, or the abuse in applying them unfairly.

Soon after your return to New York, you published a very
illiberal and unmanly handbill against the congress; for it was
certainly stepping out of the line of common civility, first to
screen your national pride by soliciting an interview with them
as private gentlemen, and in the conclusion to endeavor to
deceive the multitude by making a handbill attack on the
whole body of the congress; you got them together under one
name, and abused them under another. But the king you serve,

and the cause you support, afford you so few instances of acting the gentleman, that out of pity to your situation the congress pardoned the insult by taking no notice of it.

You say in that handbill, "that they, the congress, disavowed every purpose for reconciliation not consonant with their extravagant and inadmissible claim of independence." Why, God bless me! what have you to do with our independence? We ask no leave of yours to set it up; we ask no money of yours to support it; we can do better without your fleets and armies than with them; you may soon have enough to do to protect yourselves without being burdened with us. We are very willing to be at peace with you, to buy of you and sell to you, and, like young beginners in the world, to work for our living; therefore, why do you put yourselves out of cash, when we know you cannot spare it, and we do not desire you to run into debt? I am willing, sir, you should see your folly in every point of view I can place it in, and for that reason descend sometimes to tell you in jest what I wish you to see in earnest. But to be more serious with you, why do you say, "their independence?" To set you right, sir, we tell you, that the independency is ours, not theirs. The congress were authorized by every state on the continent to publish it to all the world, and in so doing are not to be considered as the inventors, but only as the heralds that proclaimed it, or the office from which the sense of the people received a legal form; and it was as much as any or all their heads were worth, to have treated with you on the subject of submission under any name whatever. But we know the men in whom we have trusted; can England say the same of her parliament?

I come now more particularly to your proclamation of the 30th of November last. Had you gained an entire conquest over all the armies of America, and then put forth a proclamation, offering (what you call) mercy, your conduct would have had some specious show of humanity; but to creep by surprise into a province, and there endeavor to terrify and seduce the inhabitants from their just allegiance to the rest by promises, which you neither meant, nor were able to fulfill, is both cruel and unmanly: cruel in its effects; because, unless you can keep all the ground you have marched over, how are you, in the words of your proclamation, to secure to your proselytes "the enjoyment of their property?" What is to become either of your new adopted subjects, or your old friends, the tories, in Burlington, Bordentown, Trenton, Mountholly, and many other places, where you proudly lorded it for a few days, and then fled with the precipitation of a pursued thief? What, I say, is to become of those wretches? What is to become of those who went over to you from this city and state? What more can you say to them than "shift for yourselves?" Or what more can they hope for than to wander like vagabonds over the face of the earth? You may now tell them to take their leave of America, and all that once was theirs. Recommend them, for consolation, to your master's court; there perhaps they may make a shift to live on the scraps of some dangling parasite, and choose companions among thousands like themselves. A traitor is the foulest fiend on earth.

In a political sense we ought to thank you for thus bequeathing estates to the continent; we shall soon, at this rate, be able to carry on a war without expense, and grow rich by the ill policy of Lord Howe, and the generous defection of the tories. Had you set your foot into this city, you would have bestowed estates upon us which we never thought of, by bringing forth traitors we were unwilling to suspect. But these men, you'll say, "are his majesty's most faithful subjects;" let that honor, then, be all their fortune, and let his majesty take them to himself.

I am now thoroughly disgusted with them; they live in ungrateful ease, and bend their whole minds to mischief. It seems as if God had given them over to a spirit of infidelity, and that they are open to conviction in no other line but that of punishment. It is time to have done with tarring, feathering, carting, and taking securities for their future good behavior; every sensible man must feel a conscious shame at seeing a poor fellow hawked for a show about the streets, when it is known he is only the tool of some principal villain, biassed into his offence by the force of false reasoning, or bribed thereto, through sad necessity. We dishonor ourselves by attacking such trifling characters while greater ones are suffered to escape; 'tis our duty to find *them* out, and their proper punishment would be to exile them from the continent for ever. The circle of them is not so great as some imagine; the influence of a few have tainted many who are not naturally corrupt. A continual circulation of lies among those who are not much in the way of hearing them contradicted, will in time pass for truth; and the crime lies not in the believer but the inventor. I am not for declaring war with every man that appears not so warm as myself: difference of constitution, temper, habit of speaking, and many other things, will go a great way in fixing the outward character of a man, yet simple honesty may remain at bottom. Some men have naturally a military turn, and can brave hardships and the risk of life with a cheerful face; others have not; no slavery appears to them so great as the fatigue of arms, and no terror so powerful as that of personal danger. What can we say? We cannot alter nature, neither ought we to punish the son because the father begot him in a cowardly mood. However, I believe most men have more courage than they know of, and that a little at first is enough to begin with. I knew the time when I thought that the whistling of a cannon ball would have frightened me almost to death: but I have since tried it, and find that I can stand it with as little discomposure, and, I believe, with a much easier conscience than your lordship. The same dread would return to me again were I in your situation, for my solemn belief of your cause is, that it is hellish and damnable, and, under that conviction, every thinking man's heart *must* fail him.

From a concern that a good cause should be dishonored by the least disunion among us, I said in my former paper, No. I. "That should the enemy now be expelled, I wish, with all the sincerity of a Christian, that the names of whig and tory might never more be mentioned," but there is a knot of men among us of such a venomous cast, that they will not admit even one's good wishes to act in their favor. Instead of rejoicing that heaven had, as it were, providentially preserved this city from plunder and destruction, by delivering so great a part of the enemy into our hands with so little effusion of blood, they stubbornly affected to disbelieve it till within an hour, nay, half an hour, of the prisoners arriving; and the Quakers put forth a testimony, dated the 20th of December, signed "John Pemberton," declaring their attachment to the British government.* These men are continually harping on the great sin of *our* bearing arms, but the king of Britain may lay waste the world in blood and famine, and they, poor fallen souls, have nothing to say.

In some future paper I intend to distinguish between the different kind of persons who have been denominated tories;

---

* I have ever been careful of charging offences upon whole societies of men, but as the paper referred to is put forth by an unknown set of men, who claim to themselves the right of representing the whole: and while the whole society of Quakers admit its validity by a silent acknowledgment, it is impossible that any distinction can be made by the public: and the more so, because the New York paper of the 30th of December, printed by permission of our enemies, says that "the Quakers begin to speak openly of their attachment to the British constitution." We are certain that we have many friends among them, and wish to know them.

for this I am clear in, that all are not so who have been called so, nor all men whigs who were oncethought so; and as I mean not to conceal the name of any true friend when there shall be occasion to mention him, neither will I that of an enemy, who ought to be known, let his rank, station or religion be what it may. Much pains have been taken by some to set your lordship's private character in an amiable light, but as it has chiefly been done by men who know nothing about you, and who are no ways remarkable for their attachment to us, we have no just authority for believing it. George the third has imposed upon us by the same arts, but *time*, at length, has done him justice, and the same fate may probably attend your lordship. Your avowed purpose here, is to kill, conquer, plunder, pardon, and enslave: and the ravages of your army through the Jerseys have been marked with as much barbarism as if you had openly professed yourself the prince of ruffians; not even the appearance of humanity has been preserved either on the march or the retreat of your troops; no general order that I could ever learn, has ever been issued to prevent or even forbid your troops from robbery, wherever they came; and the only instance of justice, if it can be called such, which has distinguished you for impartiality, is, that you treated and plundered all alike: what could not be carried away has been destroyed, and mahogany furniture has been deliberately laid on fire for fuel, rather than the men should be fatigued with cutting wood.* There was a time when the whigs confided much in your supposed candor, and the tories rested themselves in your favor; the experiments have now been made, and failed; in every town, nay, every cottage, in the Jerseys, where your arms have been, is a testimony

---

* As some people may doubt the truth of such wanton destruction, I think it necessary to inform them, that one of the people called Quakers, who lives at Trenton, gave me this information, at the house of Mr. Michael Hutchinson, (one of the same profession,) who lives near Trenton ferry on the Pennsylvania side, Mr. Hutchinson being present.

against you. How you may rest under this sacrifice of character I know not; but this I know, that you sleep and rise with the daily curses of thousands upon you: perhaps the misery which the tories have suffered by your proffered mercy, may give them some claim to their country's pity, and be in the end the best favor you could show them.

In a folio general-order book belonging to Col. Rhol's battalion, taken at Trenton, and now in the possession of the council of safety for the state, the following barbarous order is frequently repeated: "His excellency the *commander-in-chief* orders, that all inhabitants who shall be found with arms, not having an officer with them, shall be immediately taken and hung up." How many you may thus have privately sacrificed, we know not, and the account can only be settled in another world. Your treatment of prisoners, in order to distress them to enlist into your infernal service, is not to be equalled by any instance in Europe. Yet this is the humane Lord Howe and his brother, whom the tories and their three-quarter kindred, the Quakers, or some of them at least, have been holding up for patterns of justice and mercy!

A bad cause will ever be supported by bad means and bad men; and whoever will be at the pains of examining strictly into things, will find that one and the same spirit of oppression and impiety, more or less, governs through your whole party in both countries. Not many days ago, I accidentally fell in company with a person of this city noted for espousing your cause, and on my remarking to him, "that it appeared clear to me, by the late providential turn of affairs, that God Almighty was visible on our side," he replied, "We care nothing for that, you may have Him, and welcome; if we have but enough of the devil on our side, we shall do. " However carelessly this might be spoken, matters not, 'tis still the insensible principle that directs all your conduct, and will at last most assuredly deceive and ruin you.

If ever a nation was mad and foolish, blind to its own interest and bent on its own destruction, it is Britain. There are such things as national sins, and though the punishment of individuals may be reserved to *another* world, national punishment can only be inflicted in *this* world. Britain, as a nation, is, in my inmost belief, the greatest and most ungrateful offender against God on the face of the whole earth: blessed with all the commerce she could wish for, and furnished, by a vast extension of dominion, with the means of civilizing both the eastern and western world, she has made no other use of both than proudly to idolize her own "thunder," and rip up the bowels of whole countries for what she could get. Like Alexander, she has made war her sport, and inflicted misery for prodigality's sake. The blood of India is not yet repaid, nor the wretchedness of Africa yet requited. Of late she has enlarged her list of national cruelties, by her butcherly destruction of the Caribs of St. Vincents, and returning an answer by the sword to the meek prayer for *"Peace, liberty and safety."* These are serious things, and whatever a foolish tyrant, a debauched court, a trafficing legislature, or a blinded people may think, the national account with heaven must some day or other be settled: all countries have sooner or later been called to their reckoning; the proudest empires have sunk when the balance was struck; and Britain, like an individual penitent, must undergo her day of sorrow, and the sooner it happens to her the better: as I wish it over, I wish it to come, but withal wish that it may be as light as possible.

Perhaps your lordship has no taste for serious things; by your connexions in England I should suppose not: therefore I shall drop this part of the subject, and take it up in a line in which you will better understand me.

By what means, may I ask, do you expect to conquer America? If you could not effect it in the summer, when our army was less than yours, nor in the winter, when we had none, how are you to do it? In point or generalship you have been outwitted, and in point or fortitude outdone: your advantages turn out to your loss, and show us that it is in our power to ruin you by gifts: like a game of drafts, we can move out of *one* square to let you come in, in order that we may afterwards take two or three for one; and as we can always keep a double corner for ourselves, we can always prevent a total defeat. You cannot be so insensible, as not to see that we have two to one the advantage of you, because we conquer by a drawn game, and you lose by it. Burgoyne might have taught your lordship this knowledge; he has been long a student in the doctrine of chances.

I have no other idea of conquering countries than by subduing the armies which defend them: have you done this, or can you do it? If you have not, it would be civil in you to let your proclamations alone for the present; otherwise, you will ruin more tories by your grace and favor, than you will whigs by your arms.

Were you to obtain possession of this city, you would not know what to do with it more than to plunder it. To hold it in the manner you hold New York, would be an additional dead weight upon your hands; and if a general conquest is your object, you had better be without the city than with it. When you have defeated all our armies, the cities will fall into your hands of themselves; but to creep into them in the manner you got into Princeton, Trenton, &c., is like robbing an orchard in the night, before the fruit be ripe, and running away in the morning. Your experiment in the Jerseys is sufficient to teach you that you have something more to do than barely to get into other people's houses; and your new converts, to whom you promised all manner of protection, and seduced into new guilt by pardoning them from their former virtues, must begin to have a very contemptible opinion both of your power and your policy. Your authority in the Jerseys is now reduced to the small circle which your army occupies, and your proclamation is no where else seen unless it be to be laughed at. The mighty subduers of the continent have retreated into a nut shell, and the proud forgivers of our sins are fled from those they came to pardon; and all this at a time when they were dispatching vessel after vessel to England with the great news of every day. In short, you have managed your Jersey expedition so very dexterously, that the dead only are conquerors, because none will dispute the ground with them.

In all the wars which you have formerly been concerned in, you had only armies to contend with; in this case you have both an army and a country to combat with. In former wars, the countries followed the fate of their capitals; Canada fell with Quebec, and Minorca with Port Mahon or St. Phillips; by subduing those, the conquerors opened a way into, and became masters of the country: here it is otherwise; if you get possession of a city here, you are obliged to shut yourselves up in it, and can make no other use of it, than to spend your country's money in. This is all the advantage you have drawn from New York; and you would draw less from Philadelphia, because it requires more force to keep it, and is much further from the sea. A pretty figure you and the tories would cut in this city, with a river full of ice, and a town full of fire; for the immediate consequence of your getting here would be, that you would be cannonaded out again, and the tories be obliged to make good the damage; and this, sooner or later, will be the fate of New York.

I wish to see the city saved, not so much from military as from natural motives. 'Tis the hiding place of women and children, and Lord Howe's proper business is with our armies. When I put all the circumstances together which ought to be taken, I laugh at your notion of conquering America. Because you lived in a little country, where an army might run over the whole in a few days, and where a single company of soldiers might put a multitude to the rout, you expected to find it the same here. It is plain that you brought over with you all the narrow notions you were bred up with, and imagined that a proclamation in the king's name was to do great things; but Englishmen always travel for knowledge, and your lordship, I hope, will return, if you return at all, much wiser than you came.

We may be surprised by events we did not expect, and in that interval of recollection you may gain some temporary advantage. Such was the case a few weeks ago, but we soon ripen again into reason, collect our strength, and while you are preparing for a triumph, we come upon you with a defeat. Such it has been, and such it would be were you to try it a hundred times over. Were you to garrison the places you might march over, in order to secure their subjection, (for remember you can do it by no other means,) your army would be like a stream of water running to nothing. By the time you reached from New York to Virginia, you would be reduced to a string of drops not capable of hanging together; while we, by retreating from state to state, like a river turning back upon itself, would acquire strength in the same proportion as you lost it, and in the end be capable of overwhelming you. The country, in the mean time, would suffer, but it is a day of suffering, and we ought to expect it. What we contend for is worthy the affliction we may go through. If we get but bread to eat, and any kind of raiment to put on, we ought not only to be contented, but thankful. More than *that* we ought not to look for, and less than *that* heaven has not yet suffered us to want. He that would sell his birthright for a little *salt*, is as worthless as he who sold it for *porridge* without salt. And he that would part with it for a gay coat, or a *plain* coat, ought for ever to be a slave in buff. What are salt, sugar and finery, to the inestimable blessings of "Liberty and safety!" Or what are the inconveniences of a few months to the tributary bondage of ages? The meanest peasant in America, blest with these sentiments, is a happy man compared with a New York tory; he can eat his morsel without repining, and when he has done, can sweeten it with a repast of wholesome air; he can take his child by the hand and bless it, without feeling the conscious shame of neglecting a parent's duty.

In making these remarks I have several objects in view.

On your part they are to expose the folly of your pretended authority as a commissioner; the wickedness of your cause in general; and the impossibility of your conquering us at any rate. On the part of the public, my intention is, to show them their true and solid interest: to encourage them to their own good, to remove the fears and falsities which bad men have spread, and weak men have encouraged; and to excite in all men a love for union, and a cheerfulness for duty. I shall submit one more case to you respecting your conquest of this country, and then proceed to new observations.

Suppose our armies in every part of this continent were immediately to disperse, every man to his home, or where else he might be safe, and engage to re-assemble again on a certain future day; it is clear that you would then have no army to contend with, yet you would be as much at a loss in that case as you are now; you would be afraid to send your troops in parties over the continent, either to disarm, or prevent us from assembling, lest they should not return; and while you kept them together, having no army of ours to dispute with, you could not call it a conquest; you might furnish out a pompous page in the *London Gazette* or a New York paper, but when we returned at the appointed time, you would have the same work to do that you had at first.

It has been the folly of Britain to suppose herself more powerful than she really is, and by that means has arrogated to herself a rank in the world she is not entitled to: for more than this century past she has not been able to carry on a war without foreign assistance. In Marlborough's campaigns, and from that day to this, the number of German troops and officers assisting her have been about equal with her own; ten thousand Hessians were sent to England last war to protect her from a French invasion; and she would have cut but a poor figure in her Canadian and West-Indian expeditions, had not America been lavish both of her money and men to help her along. The only instance in which she was engaged singly, that I can recollect, was against the rebellion in Scotland, in the years 1745 and 1746, and in that, out of three battles, she was twice beaten, till by thus reducing their numbers, (as we shall yours,) and taking a supply ship that was coming to Scotland with clothes, arms and money, (as we have often done,) she was at last enabled to defeat them. England was never famous by land; her officers have generally been suspected of cowardice, have more of the air of a dancing master than a soldier, and by the samples which we have taken prisoners, we give the preference to ourselves. Her strength, of late, has lain in her extravagance; but as her finances and credit are now low, her sinews in that line begin to fail fast. As a nation she is the poorest in Europe; for were the whole kingdom, and all that is in it, to be put up for sale like the estate of a bankrupt, it would not fetch as much as she owes; yet this thoughtless wretch must go to war, and with the avowed design, too, of making us beasts of burden, to support her in riot and debauchery, and to assist her afterwards in distressing those nations who are now our best friends. This ingratitude may suit a tory, or the unchristian peevishness of a fallen Quaker, but none else.

'Tis the unhappy temper of the English to be pleased with any war, right or wrong, be it but successful; but they soon grow discontented with ill fortune, and it is an even chance that they are as clamorous for peace next summer, as the king and his ministers were for war last winter. In this natural view of things, your lordship stands in a very critical situation: your whole character is now staked upon your laurels; if they wither, you wither with them; if they flourish, you cannot live long to look at them; and at any rate, the black account hereafter is not far off. What lately appeared to us misfortunes, were only blessings in disguise; and the seeming advantages on your side have turned out to our profit. Even our loss of this city, as far as we can see, might be a principal gain to us: the more surface you spread over, the thinner you will be, and the easier wiped away; and our consolation under that apparent disaster would be, that the estates of the tories would become securities for the repairs. In short, there is no old ground we can fail upon, but some new foundation rises again to support us. "We have put, sir, our hands to the plough, and cursed be he that looketh back."

Your king, in his speech to parliament last spring, declared, "That he had no doubt but the great force they had enabled him to send to America, would effectually reduce the rebellious colonies." It has not, neither can it; but it has done just enough to lay the foundation of its own next year's ruin. You are sensible that you left England in a divided, distracted state of politics, and, by the command you had here, you became a principal prop in the court party; their fortunes rest on yours; by a single express you can fix their value with the public, and the degree to which their spirits shall rise or fall; they are in your hands as stock, and you have the secret of the *alley* with you. Thus situated and connected, you become the unintentional mechanical instrument of your own and their overthrow. The king and his ministers put conquest out of doubt, and the credit of both depended on the proof. To support them in the interim, it was necessary that you should make the most of every thing, and we can tell by Hugh Game's New York paper what the complexion of the *London Gazette* is. With such a list of victories the nation cannot expect you will ask new supplies; and to confess your want of them, would give the lie to your triumphs, and impeach the king and his ministers of treasonable deception. If you make the necessary demand at home, your party sinks; if you make it not, you sink yourself; to ask it now is too late, and to ask it before was too soon, and unless it arrive quickly will be of no use. In short, the part you have to act, cannot be acted; and I am fully persuaded that all you have to trust to is, to do the best you can with what force you have got, or little more. Though we have greatly exceeded you in point of generalship and bravery of men, yet, as a people, we have not entered into the full soul of enterprise; for I, who know England and the disposition of the people well, am confident, that it is easier for us to effect a revolution there, than you a conquest here; a few thousand men landed in England with the declared design of deposing the present king, bringing his ministers to trial, and setting up the Duke of Gloucester in his stead, would assuredly carry their point, while you were grovelling here ignorant of the matter. As I send all my papers to England, this, like *Common Sense*, will find its way there; and though it may put one party on their guard, it will inform the other, and the nation in general, of our design to help them.

Thus far, sir, I have endeavored to give you a picture of present affairs: you may draw from it what conclusions you please. I wish as well to the true prosperity of England as you can, but I consider INDEPENDENCE *as America's natural right and interest*, and never could see any real disservice it would be to Britain. If an English merchant receives an order, and is paid for it, it signifies nothing to him who governs the country. This is my creed of politics. If I have any where expressed myself over-warmly, 'tis from a fixed, immovable hatred I have, and ever had, to cruel men and cruel measures. I have likewise an aversion to monarchy, as being too debasing to the dignity of man; but I never troubled others with my notions till very lately, nor ever published a syllable in England in my life. What I write is pure nature, and my pen and my soul have ever gone together. My writings I have always given away, reserving only the expense of printing and paper, and sometimes not even that. I never courted either fame or interest, and my manner of life, to those who know it, will justify what I say. My study is to be useful, and if your lordship loves mankind as well as I do, you would, seeing you cannot conquer us, cast about and lend your hand towards accomplishing a peace. Our independence, with God's blessing, we will maintain against all the world; but as we wish to avoid evil ourselves, we wish not to inflict it on others. I am never over inquisitive into the secrets of the cabinet, but I have some notion, that if you neglect the present opportunity, that it will not be in our power to make a separate peace with you afterwards; for whatever treaties or alliances we form, we shall most faithfully abide by; wherefore you may be deceived if you think you can make it with us at any time. A lasting independent peace is my wish, end and aim; and to accomplish that, *"I pray God the* Americans *may never be defeated, and I trust while they have good officers, and are well commanded,"* and willing to be commanded, *"that they* NEVER WILL."

COMMON SENSE.
Philadelphia, Jan. 13, 1777.

THE CRISIS
NUMBER III

IN the progress of politics, as in the common occurrences of life, we are not only apt to forget the ground we have travelled over, but frequently neglect to gather up experience as we go. We expend, if I may so say, the knowledge of every day on the circumstances that produce it, and journey on in search of new matter and new refinements: but as it is pleasant and sometimes useful to look back, even to the first periods of infancy, and trace the turns and windings through which we have passed, so we may likewise derive many advantages by halting a while in our political career; and taking a review of the wondrous complicated labyrinth of little more than yesterday.

Truly may we say, that never did men grow old in so short a time! We have crowded the business of an age into the compass of a few months, and have been driven through such a rapid succession of things, that for the want of leisure to think, we unavoidably wasted knowledge as we came, and have left nearly as much behind us as we brought with us: but the road is yet rich with the fragments, and before we fully lose sight of them, will repay us for the trouble of stopping to pick them up.

Were a man to be totally deprived of memory, he would be incapable of forming any just opinion; every thing about him would seem a chaos; he would have even his own history to ask from every one; and by not knowing how the world went in his absence, he would be at a loss to know how it *ought* to go on when he recovered, or rather, returned to it again. In like manner, though in a less degree, a too great inattention to past occurrences retards and bewilders our judgment in every thing; while, on the contrary, by comparing what is past with what is present, we frequently hit on the true character of both, and become wise with very little trouble. It is a kind of counter-march, by which we get into the rear of time, and mark the movements and meaning of things as we make our return. There are certain circumstances, which, at the time of their happening, are a kind of riddles and as every riddle is to be followed by its answer, so those kind of circumstances will be followed by their events, and those events are always the true solution. A considerable space of time may lapse between, and unless we continue our observations from the one to the other, the harmony of them will pass away unnoticed; but the misfortune is, that partly from the pressing necessity of some instant things, and partly from the impatience of our own tempers, we are frequently in such a hurry to make out the meaning of every thing as fast as it happens, that we thereby never truly understand it; and not only start new difficulties to ourselves by so doing, but, as it were, embarrass Providence in her good designs.

I have been civil in stating this fault on a large scale, for, as it now stands, it does not appear to be levelled against any particular set of men; but were it to be refined a little further, it might afterwards be applied to the tories with a degree of striking propriety: those men have been remarkable for drawing sudden conclusions from single facts. The least apparent mishap on our side, or the least seeming advantage on the part of the enemy, have determined with them the fate of a whole campaign. By this hasty judgment they have converted a retreat into a defeat; mistook generalship for error; while every little advantage purposely given the enemy, either to weaken their strength by dividing it, embarrass their councils by multiplying their objects, or to secure a greater post by the surrender of a less, has been instantly magnified into a conquest. Thus, by quartering ill policy upon ill principles, they have frequently promoted the cause they designed to injure, and injured that which they intended to promote. It is probable the campaign may open before this number comes from the press. The enemy have long lain idle, and amused themselves with carrying on the war by proclamations only. While they continue their delay our strength increases, and were they to move to action now, it is a circumstantial proof that they have no reinforcement coming; wherefore, in either case, the comparative advantage will be ours. Like a wounded, disabled whale, they want only time and room to die in; and though in the agony of their exit, it may be unsafe to live within the flapping of their tail, yet every hour shortens their date, and lessens their power of mischief. If any thing happens while this number is in press, it will afford me a subject for the last pages of it. At present I am tired of waiting; and as neither the enemy, nor the state of politics have *yet* produced any thing new, I am thereby left in the field of general matter, undirected by any striking or particular object. This *Crisis*, therefore, will be made up rather of variety than novelty, and consist more of things useful than things wonderful.

The success of the cause, the union of the people, and the means of supporting and securing both, are points which cannot be too much attended to. He who doubts of the former is a desponding coward, and he who willfully disturbs the latter is a traitor. Their characters are easily fixed, and under these short descriptions I leave them for the present.

One of the greatest degrees of sentimental union which America ever knew, was in denying the right of the British parliament *"to bind the colonies in all cases whatsoever."* The declaration is, in its form, an almighty one, and is the loftiest stretch of arbitrary power that ever one set of men, or one country claimed over another. Taxation was nothing more than the putting the declared right into practice; and this failing, recourse was had to arms, as a means to establish both the right *and* the practice, or to answer a worse purpose, which will be mentioned in the course of this number. And in order to repay themselves the expense of an army, and to profit by their own injustice, the colonies were, by another law, declared to be in a state of actual rebellion, and of consequence all property therein would fall to the conquerors.

The colonies, on their part, *first*, denied the right; *secondly*, they suspended the use of taxable articles, and petitioned against the practice of taxation: and these failing, they, *thirdly*, defended their property by force, as soon as it was forcibly invaded, and in answer to the declaration of rebellion and non-protection, published their declaration of independence and right of self-protection.

These, in a few words, are different stages of the quarrel; and the parts are so intimately and necessarily connected with each other as to admit of no separation. A person, to use a trite phrase, must be a whig or a tory in the lump. His feelings, as a man, may be wounded; his charity, as a Christian, may be moved; but his political principles must go through all the cases on one side or the other. He cannot be a whig in *this* stage, and a tory in *that*. If he says he is against the united independence of the continent, he is to all intents and purposes against her in all the rest; because *this last* comprehends the whole. And he may just as well say, that Britain was right in declaring us rebels; right in taxing us; and right in declaring her "*right to bind the colonies in all cases whatsoever.*" It signifies nothing what neutral ground, of his own creating, he may skulk upon for shelter, for the quarrel in no stage of it hath afforded any such ground; and either we or Britain are absolutely right or absolutely wrong through the whole.

Britain, like a gamester nearly ruined, hath now put all her losses into one bet, and is playing a desperate game for the total. If she wins it, she wins from *me* my life; she wins the continent as the forfeited property of rebels; the right of taxing those that are left as reduced subjects; and the power of binding them slaves: and the single die which determines this unparalleled event is, whether we support our independence or she overturn it. This is coming to the point at once. Here is the touchstone to try men by. *He that is not a supporter of the independent states of America, in the same degree that his religious and political principles would suffer him to support the government of any other country, of which he called himself a subject, is, in the American sense of the word,* A TORY; *and the instant that he endeavors to bring his toryism into practice, he becomes* A TRAITOR. The first can only be detected by a general test, and the law hath already provided for the latter.

It is unnatural and impolitic to admit men who would root up our independence to have any share in our legislation, either as electors or representatives; because the support of our independence rests, in a great measure, on the vigor and purity of our public bodies. Would Britain, even in time of peace, much less in war, suffer an election to be carried by men who professed themselves to be not her subjects, or allow such to sit in parliament? Certainly not.

But there are a certain species of tories with whom conscience or principle hath nothing to do, and who are so from avarice only. Some of the first fortunes on the continent, on the part of the whigs, are staked on the issue of our present measures. And shall disaffection only be rewarded with security?

Can any thing be a greater inducement to a miserly man, than the hope of making his mammon safe? And though the scheme be fraught with every character of folly, yet, so long as he supposes, that by doing nothing materially criminal against America on one part, and by expressing his private disapprobation against independence, as palliative with the enemy on the other part, he stands thereby in a safe line between both; while, I say, this ground be suffered to remain, craft, and the spirit of avarice, will point it out, and men will not be wanting to fill up this most contemptible of all characters.

These men, ashamed to own the sordid cause from whence their disaffection springs, add thereby meanness to meanness, by endeavoring to shelter themselves under the mask of hypocrisy; that is, they had rather be thought to be tories from *some kind of principle*, than tories by having *no principle at all*. But till such time as they can show some real reason, natural, political, or conscientious, on which their objections to independence are founded, we are not obliged to give them credit for being tories of the first stamp, but must set them down as tories of the last.

In the second number of the *Crisis*, I endeavored to show the impossibility of the enemy's making any conquest of America, that nothing was wanting on our part but patience and perserverance, and that, with these virtues, our success, as far as human speculation could discern, seemed as certain as fate. But as there are many among us, who, influenced by others, have regularly gone back from the principles they once held, in proportion as we have gone forward; and as it is the unfortunate lot of many a good man to live within the neighborhood of disaffected ones; I shall, therefore, for the sake of confirming the one and recovering the other, endeavor, in the space of a page or two, to go over some of the leading principles in support of independence. It is a much pleasanter task to prevent vice than to punish it, and, however our tempers may be gratified by resentment, or our national expenses eased by forfeited estates, harmony and friendship is, nevertheless, the happiest condition a country can be blest with.

The principal arguments in support of independence may be comprehended under the four following heads.

First, The natural right to the continent to independence.

Second, Her interest in being independent.

Third, The necessity,—and

Fourth, The moral advantages arising therefrom.

First. The natural right of the continent to independence, is a point which never yet was called in question. It will not even admit of a debate. To deny such a right, would be a kind of atheism against nature: and the best answer to such an objection would be, "*The fool hath said in his heart there is no God.*"

Second. The interest of the continent in being independent is a point as clearly right as the former. America, by her own internal industry, and unknown to all the powers of Europe, was, at the beginning of the dispute, arrived at a pitch of greatness, trade and population, beyond which it was the interest of Britain not to suffer her to pass, lest she should grow too powerful to be kept subordinate. She began to view this country with the same uneasy malicious eye, with which a covetous guardian would view his ward, whose estate he had been enriching himself by for twenty years, and saw him just arriving at manhood. And America owes no more to Britain for her present maturity, than the ward would to his guardian for being twenty-one years of age. That America hath flourished *at the time* she was under the government of Britain, is true; but there is every natural reason to believe, that had she been an independent country from the first settlement thereof, uncontrolled by any foreign power, free to make her own laws, regulate and encourage her own commerce, she had by this time been of much greater worth than now. The case is simply this: the first settlers in the different colonies were left to shift for themselves, unnoticed and unsupported by any European government: but as the tyranny and persecution of the old world daily drove numbers to the new, and as, by the favor of heaven on their industry and perseverance, they grew into importance, so, in a like degree, they became an object of profit to the greedy eyes of Europe. It was impossible, in this state of infancy, however thriving and promising, that they could resist the power of any armed invader that should seek to bring them under his authority. In this situation, Britain thought it worth her while to claim them, and the continent received and acknowledged the claimer. It was, in reality, of no very great importance who was her master, seeing, that from the force and ambition of the different powers of Europe, she must, till she acquired strength enough to assert her own right, acknowledge some one. As well, perhaps, Britain as another; and it might have been as well to have been under the states of Holland as any. The same hopes of engrossing and profiting by her trade, by not oppressing it too much, would have operated alike with any master, and produced to the colonies the same effects. The clamor of protection, likewise, was all a farce; because, in order to make *that* protection necessary, she must first, by her own quarrels, create us enemies. Hard times, indeed!

To know whether it be the interest of the continent to be independent, we need only ask this easy, simple question: Is it the interest of a man to be a boy all his life? The answer to one will be the answer to both. America hath been one continued scene of legislative contention from the first king's representative to the last; and this was unavoidably founded in the natural opposition of interest between the old country and the new. A governor sent from England, or receiving his authority therefrom, ought never to have been considered in any other light than that of a genteel commissioned spy, whose private business was information, and his public business a kind of civilized oppression. In the first of these characters he was to watch the tempers, sentiments and disposition of the people, the growth of trade, and the increase of private fortunes; and, in the latter, to suppress all such acts of the assemblies, however beneficial to the people, which did not directly or indirectly throw some increase of power or profit into the hands of those that sent him.

America, till now, could never be called a *free country*, because her legislation depended on the will of a man three thousand miles distant, whose interest was in opposition to ours, and who, by a single "no," could forbid what law he pleased.

The freedom of trade, likewise, is, to a trading country, an article of such importance, that the principal source of wealth depends upon it; and it is impossible that any country can flourish, as it otherwise might do, whose commerce is engrossed, cramped and fettered by the laws and mandates of another—yet these evils, and more than I can here enumerate, the continent has suffered by being under the government of England. By an independence we clear the whole at once—put an end to the business of unanswered petitions and fruitless remonstrances—exchange Britain for Europe—shake hands with the world—live at peace with the world—and trade to any market where we can buy and sell.

Third. The necessity, likewise, of being independent, even before it was declared, became so evident and important, that the continent ran the risk of being ruined every day that she delayed it. There was reason to believe that Britain would endeavor to make a European matter of it, and, rather than lose the whole, would dismember it, like Poland, and dispose of her several claims to the highest bidder. Genoa, failing in her attempts to reduce Corsica, made a sale of it to the French, and such traffics have been common in the old world. We had at that time no ambassador in any part of Europe, to counteract her negotiations, and by that means, she had the range of every foreign court uncontradicted on our part. We even knew nothing of the treaty for the Hessians till it was concluded, and the troops ready to embark. Had we been independent before, we had probably prevented her obtaining them. We had no credit abroad, because of our rebellious dependency. Our ships could claim no protection in foreign ports, because we afforded them no justifiable reason for granting it to us. The calling ourselves subjects, and at the same time fighting against the power which we acknowledged, was a dangerous precedent to all Europe. If the grievances justified the taking up arms, they justified our separation; if they did not justify our separation, neither could they justify our taking up arms. All Europe was interested in reducing us as rebels, and all Europe (or the greatest part at least) is interested in supporting us as independent states. At home our condition was still worse; our currency had no foundation, and the fall of it would have ruined whig and tory alike. We had no other law than a kind of moderated passion; no other civil power than an honest mob; and no other protection than the temporary attachment of one man to another. Had independence been delayed a few months longer, this continent would have been plunged into irrecoverable confusion: some violent for it, some against it, till, in the general cabal, the rich would have been ruined, and the poor destroyed. It is to independence that every tory owes the present safety which he lives in; for by *that*, and *that only*, we emerged from a state of dangerous suspense, and became a regular people.

The necessity, likewise, of being independent, had there been no rupture between Britain and America, would, in a little time, have brought one on. The increasing importance of commerce, the weight and perplexity of legislation, and the entangled state of European politics, would daily have shown to the continent the impossibility of continuing subordinate; for, after the coolest reflections on the matter, *this must* be allowed, that Britain was too jealous of America to govern it justly; too ignorant of it to govern it well; and too far distant from it to govern it at all.

Fourth. But what weigh most with all men of serious reflection are, the *moral advantages* arising from independence: war and desolation have become the trade of the old world; and America neither could, nor can be under the government of Britain without becoming a sharer of her guilt, and a partner in all the dismal commerce of death. The spirit of duelling, extended on a national scale, is a proper character for European wars. They have seldom any other motive than pride, or any other object than fame. The conquerors and the conquered are generally ruined alike, and the chief difference at last is, that the one marches home with his honors, and the other without them. 'Tis the natural temper of the English to fight for a feather, if they suppose *that feather* to be an affront; and America, without the right of asking why, must have abetted in every quarrel, and abided by its fate. It is a shocking situation to live in, that one country must be brought into all the wars of another, whether the measure be right or wrong, or whether she will or not; yet this, in the fullest extent, was, and ever would be, the unavoidable consequence of the connection. Surely the Quakers forgot their own principles, when, in their late Testimony, they called *this connection*, with these miitary and miserable appendages hanging to it—"*the happy constitution*."

Britain, for centuries past, had been nearly fifty years out of every hundred at war with some power or other. It certainly ought to be a conscientious as well as political consideration with America, not to dip her hands in the bloody work of Europe. Our situation affords us a retreat from their cabals, and the present happy union of the states bids fair for extirpating the future use of arms from one quarter of the world; yet such have been the irreligious politics of the present leaders of the Quakers, that, for the sake of they scarce know what, they would cut off every hope of such a blessing by tying this continent to Britain, like Hector to the chariot wheel of Achilles, to be dragged through all the miseries of endless European wars.

The connection, viewed from this ground, is distressing to every man who has the feelings of humanity. By having Britain for our master, we became enemies to the greatest part of Europe, and they to us: and the consequence was war inevitable. By being our own masters, independent of any foreign one, we have Europe for our friends, and the prospect of an endless peace among ourselves. Those who were advocates for the British government over these colonies, were obliged to limit both their arguments, and their ideas to the period of an European peace only: the moment Britain became plunged in war, every supposed convenience to us vanished, and all we could hope for was *not to be ruined*. Could this be a desirable condition for a young country to be in?

Had the French pursued their fortune immediately after the defeat of Braddock's last war, this city and province had then experienced the woeful calamities of being a British subject. A scene of the same kind might happen again; for America, considered as a subject to the crown of Britain, would ever have been the seat of war and the bone of contention between the two powers.

On the whole, if the future expulsion of arms from one quarter of the world would be a desirable object to a peaceable man;—if the freedom of trade to every part of it can engage the attention of a man of business;—if the support or fall of millions of currency can affect our interests;—if the entire possession of estates, by cutting off the lordly claims of Britain over the soil, deserves the regard of landed property;—and if the right of making our own laws, uncontrolled by the royal or ministerial spies or mandates, be worthy our care as freemen ;—then are all men interested in the support of independence; and may he that supports it not, be driven from the blessing, to live unpitied beneath the servile sufferings of scandalous subjection!

We have been amused with the tales of ancient wonders; we have read and wept over the histories of other nations; applauded, censured, or pitied, as their cases affected us.—The fortitude and patience of the sufferers—the justness of their cause—the weight of their oppressions and oppressors—the object to be saved or lost—with all the consequences of a defeat or a conquest—have, in the hour of sympathy, bewitched our hearts, and chained it to their fate: but where is the power that ever made war upon petitioners? Or where is the war on which a world was staked till now?

We may not, perhaps, be wise enough to make all the advantages we ought of our independence; but they are, nevertheless, marked and presented to us with every character of

great and *good*, and worthy the hand of him who sent them. I
look through the present trouble to a time of tranquillity, when
we shall have it in our power to set an example of peace to all
the world. Were the Quakers really impressed and influenced
by the quiet principles they profess to hold, they would, however they might disapprove the means, be the first of all men
to approve of *independence*, because, by separating ourselves
from the cities of Sodom and Gomorrah, it affords an opportunity never given to man before, of carrying their favorite principle of peace into general practice, by establishing governments that shall hereafter exist without wars. O! ye fallen,
cringing, priest and Pemberton-ridden people! What more can
we say of ye than that a religious Quaker is a valuable character, and a political Quaker a real Jesuit?

Having thus gone over some of the principal points in support of independence, I must now request the reader to return
back with me to the period when it first began to be a public
doctrine, and to examine the progress it has made among the
various classes of men. The era I mean to begin at, is the
breaking out of hostilities, April 19th, 1775. Until this event
happened, the continent seemed to view the dispute as a kind
of law-suit for a matter of right, litigating between the old
country and the new; and she felt the same kind and degree of
horror, as if she had seen an oppressive plaintiff, at the head of
a band of ruffians, enter the court, while the cause was before
it, and put the judge, the jury, the defendant and his counsel, to
the sword. Perhaps a more heart-felt convulsion never reached
a country with the same degree of power and rapidity before,
and never may again. Pity for the sufferers, mixed with
indignation at the violence, and heightened with apprehensions
of undergoing the same fate made the affair of Lexington the
affair of the continent. Every part of it felt the shock, and all

vibrated together. A general promotion of sentiment took place: those who had drank deeply into whiggish principles, that is, the right and necessity not only of opposing, but wholly setting aside the power of the crown as soon as it became practically dangerous (for in theory it was always so) stepped into the first stage of independence; while another class of whigs, equally sound in principle, but not so sanguine in enterprise, attached themselves the stronger to the cause, and fell close in with the rear of the former; their partition was a mere point. Numbers of the moderate men, whose chief fault, *at that time*, arose from their entertaining a better opinion of Britain than she deserved, convinced now of their mistake, gave her up, and publicly declared themselves good whigs. While the tories, seeing it was no longer a laughing matter, either sunk into silent obscurity, or contented themselves with coming forth and abusing General Gage: not a single advocate appeared to justify the action of that day; it seemed to appear to every one with the same magnitude, struck every one with the same force, and created in every one the same abhorrence. From this period we may date the growth of independence.

If the many circumstances which happened at this memorable time, be taken in one view, and compared with each other, they will justify a conclusion which seems not to have been attended to, I mean a fixed design in the king and ministry of driving America into arms, in order that they might be furnished with a pretence for seizing the whole continent, as the immediate property of the crown. A noble plunder for hungry courtiers!

It ought to be remembered, that the first petition from the congress was at this time unanswered on the part of the British king. That the motion, called Lord North's motion, of the 20th of February, 1775, arrived in America the latter end of March. This motion was to be laid by several governors, then in being, before the assembly of each province; and the first assembly before which it was laid, was the assembly of Pennsylvania, in *May* following. This being a just state of the case, I then ask, why were hostilities commenced between the time of passing the resolve in the House of Commons, of the 20th of February, and the time of the assemblies meeting to deliberate upon it? Degrading and infamous as that motion was, there is, nevertheless, reason to believe that the king and his adherents were afraid the colonies would agree to it, and lest they should, took effectual care they should not, by provoking them with hostilities in the interim. They had not the least doubt at that time of conquering America at one blow; and what they expected to get by a conquest being infinitely greater than any thing they could hope to get either by taxation or accommodation, they seemed determined to prevent even the possibility of hearing each other, lest America should disappoint their greedy hopes of the whole, by listening even to their own terms. On the one hand they refused to hear the petition of the continent, and on the other hand took effectual care the continent should not hear them.

That the motion of the 20th of February and the orders for commencing hostilities were both concerted by the same person or persons, and not the latter by General Gage, as was falsely imagined at first, is evident from an extract of a letter of his to the administration, read among other papers in the House of Commons, in which he informs his masters, *"That though their idea of his disarming certain counties was a right one, yet it required him to be master of the country, in order to enable him to execute it."* This was prior to the commencement of hostilities, and consequently before the motion of the 20th of February could be deliberated on by the several assemblies.

Perhaps it may be asked, why was the motion passed, if there was at the same time a plan to aggravate Americans not to listen to it? Lord North assigned one reason himself, which, was *a hope of dividing them*. This was publicly tempting them to reject it; that if, in case the injury of arms should fail in provoking them sufficiently, the insult of such a declaration might fill it up. But by passing the motion and getting it afterwards rejected in America, it enabled them, in their wretched idea of politics, among other things, to hold up the colonies to foreign powers, with every possible mark of disobedience and rebellion. They had applied to those powers not to supply the continent with arms, ammunition, &c., and it was necessary they should incense them against us, by assigning on their own part some seeming reputable reason why. By dividing, it had a tendency to weaken the states, and likewise to perplex the adherents of America in England. But the principal scheme, and that which has marked their character in every part of their conduct, was a design of precipitating the colonies into a state which they might afterwards deem rebellion, and, under that pretence, put an end to all future complaints, petitions and remonstrances, by seizing the whole at once. They had ravaged one part of the globe, till it could glut them no longer; their prodigality required new plunder, and through the East India article *tea* they hoped to transfer their rapine from that quarter of the world to this. Every designed quarrel had its pretence: and the same barbarian avarice accompanied the *plant* to America, which ruined the country that produced it.

That men never turn rogues without turning fools is a maxim, sooner or later, universally true. The commencement of hostilities, being in the beginning of April, was, of all times the worst chosen; the congress were to meet the tenth of May following, and the distress the continent felt at this unparalleled outrage gave a stability to *that body*, which no other circumstance could have done. It suppressed, too, all inferior debates, and bound them together by a necessitous affection, without giving them time to differ, upon trifles. The suffering, likewise, softened the whole body of the people into a degree of pliability, which laid the principal foundation-stone of union, order and government; and which, at any other time, might only have fretted and then faded away unnoticed and unimproved: but Providence, who best knows how to time her misfortunes as well as her immediate favor, chose this to be the time: And who dare dispute it?

It did not seem the disposition of the people, at this crisis, to heap petition upon petition, while the former remained unanswered: the measure, however, was carried in Congress, and a second petition was sent; of which I shall only remark that it was submissive even to a dangerous fault, because the prayer of it appealed solely to, what it called the prerogative of the crown, while the matter in dispute was confessed to be constitutional. But even this petition, flattering as it was, was still not so harmonious as the chink of cash, and consequently not sufficiently grateful to the tyrant and his ministry. From every circumstance it is evident, that it was the determination of the British court to have nothing to do with America but to conquer it fully and absolutely. They were certain of success, and the field of battle was to be the only place of treaty. I am confident there are thousands and tens of thousands in America who wonder *now* that they should ever have thought otherwise; but the sin of that day was the sin of civility, yet it operated against our present good in the same manner that a civil opinion of the devil would against our future peace.

Independence was a doctrine scarce and rare, even towards the conclusion of the year 1775; all our politics had been founded on the hope or expectation of making the matter up—a hope, which, though general on the side of America, had never entered the head or heart of the British court. Their hope was conquest and confiscation. Good heavens! what volumes of thanks does America owe to Britain? What infinite obligation to the tool that fills, with paradoxical vacancy, the throne! Nothing but the sharpest essence of villainy, compounded with the strongest distillation of folly, could have produced a menstruum that would have effected a separation. The Congress in 1774, administered an abortive medicine to independence, by prohibiting the importation of goods, and the succeeding congress rendered the dose still more dangerous by continuing it. Had independence been a settled system with America, (as Britain has advanced,) she ought to have *doubled* her importation, and prohibited in some degree her exportation. And this single circumstance is sufficient to acquit America before any jury of nations, of having a continental plan of independence in view: a charge which, had it been true, would have been honorable, but is so grossly false, that either the amazing ignorance, or the wilful dishonesty of the British court, is effectually proved by it.

The second petition, like the first, produced no answer; it was scarcely acknowledged to have been received; the British court were too determined in their villainy even to act it artfully, and in their rage for conquest neglected the necessary subtleties for obtaining it. They might have divided, distracted and played a thousand tricks with us, had they been as cunning as they were cruel.

This last indignity gave a new spring to independence. Those who knew the savage obstinacy of the king, and the jobbing, gambling spirit of the court, predicted the fate of the petition, as soon as it was sent from America; for the men being known, their measures were easily foreseen. As politicians we ought not so much to ground our hopes on the reasonableness of the thing we ask, as on the reasonableness of the person of whom we ask it: Who would expect discretion from a fool, candor from a tyrant, or justice from a villain?

As every prospect of accommodation seemed now to fail fast, men began to think seriously on the matter; and their reason being thus stripped of the false hope which had long encompassed it, became approachable by fair debate. Yet still the bulk of the people hesitated. They startled at the novelty of independence, without once considering that our getting into arms at first was a more extraordinary novelty, and that all other nations had gone through the work of independence before us. They doubted likewise the ability of the continent to support it, without reflecting that it required the same force to obtain an accommodation by arms as an indedependence. If the one was acquirable, the other was the same; because, to accomplish either, it was necessary that our strength should be too great for Britain to subdue; and it was too unreasonable to suppose, that with the power of being masters, we should submit to be servants.* Their caution at this time was exceedingly misplaced: for if they were able to defend their property

---

* In this state of political suspense the pamphlet *Common Sense* made its appearance, and the success it met with does not become me to mention. Dr. Franklin, Mr. Samuel and John Adams, were severally spoken of as the supposed author. I had not, at that time, the pleasure either of personally knowing or being known to the last two gentlemen. The favor of Dr. Franklin's friendship I possessed in England, and my introduction to this part of the world was through his patronage. I happened, when a school-boy, to pick up a pleasing natural history of Virginia, and my inclination from that day of seeing the western side of the Atlantic never left me. In October, 1775, Dr. Franklin proposed giving me such materials as were in his hands, towards completing a history of the present transactions, and seemed desirous of having the first volume out the next spring. I had then formed the outlines of *Common Sense*, and finished nearly the first part; and as I supposed the doctor's design in getting out a history, was to open the new year with a new system, I expected to surprise him with a production on that subject, much earlier than he had thought of; and without informing him what I was doing, got it ready for the press as fast as I conveniently could, and sent him the first pamphlet that was printed off.

and maintain their rights by arms, they, consequently, were able to defend and support their independence; and in proportion as these men saw the necessity and correctness of the measure, they honestly and openly declared and adopted it, and the part they have acted since, has done them honor and fully established their characters. Error in opinion has this peculiar advantage with it, that the foremost point of the contrary ground may at any time be reached by the sudden exertion of a thought; and it frequently happens in sentimental differences, that some striking circumstance, or some forcible reason quickly conceived, will effect in an instant what neither argument nor example could produce in an age.

I find it impossible in the small compass I am limited to, to trace out the progress which independence has made on the minds of the different classes of men, and the several reasons by which they were moved. With some, it was a passionate abhorrence against the king of England and his ministry, as a set of savages and brutes; and these men, governed by the agony of a wounded mind, were for trusting every thing to hope and heaven, and bidding defiance at once. With others, it was a growing conviction that the scheme of the British court was to create, ferment and drive on a quarrel, for the sake of confiscated plunder: and men of this cast ripened into independence in proportion as the evidence increased. While a third class conceived it was the true interest of America, internally and externally, to be her own master, and gave their support to independence, step by step, as they saw her abilities to maintain it enlarge. With many, it was a compound of all these reasons; while those who were too callous to be reached by either, remained, and still remain tories.

The *legal necessity* of being independent, with several collateral reasons, is pointed out in an elegant masterly manner, in a charge to the grand jury for the district of Charleston, by the Hon. William Henry Drayton, chief justice of South Carolina. This performance, and the address of the convention of New York, are pieces, in my humble opinion, of the first rank in America.

The principal causes why independence has not been so universally supported as it ought, are *fear* and *indolence*, and the causes why it has been opposed, are *avarice, down-right villainy,* and *lust of personal power.* There is not such a being in America as a tory from conscience; some secret defect or other is interwoven in the character of all those, be they men or women, who can look with patience on the brutality, luxury and debauchery of the British court, and the violations of their army here. A woman's virtue must sit very lightly on her who can even hint a favorable sentiment in their behalf. It is remarkable that the whole race of prostitutes in New York were tories; and the schemes for supporting the tory cause in this city, for which several are now in jail, and one hanged, were concerted and carried on in common bawdy-houses, assisted by those who kept them.

The connection between vice and meanness is a fit subject for satire, but when the satire is a fact, it cuts with the irresistible power of a diamond. If a Quaker, in defence of his just rights, his property, and the chastity of his house, takes up a musket, he is expelled the meeting; but the present king of England, who seduced and took into keeping a sister of their society, is reverenced and supported by repeated Testimonies, while the friendly noodle from whom she was taken (and who is now in this city) continues a drudge in the service of his rival, as if proud of being cuckolded by a creature called a king.

Our support and success depend on such a variety of men

and circumstances, that every one, who does but wish well, is of some use. There are men who have a strange aversion to arms, yet have hearts to risk every shilling in the cause, or in support of those who have better talents for defending it. Nature, in the arrangement of mankind, has fitted some for every service in life. Were all soldiers, all would starve and go naked, and were none soldiers, all would be slaves. As *disaffection* to independence is the badge of a tory, so *affection* to it is the mark of a whig: and the different services of the whigs, down from those who nobly contribute every thing, to those who have nothing to render but their wishes, tend all to the same centre, though with different degrees of merit and ability. The larger we make the circle, the more we shall harmonize, and the stronger we shall be. All we want to shut out is disaffection, and *that excluded*, we must accept from each other such duties as we are best fitted to bestow. A narrow system of politics, like a narrow system of religion, is calculated only to sour the temper, and be at variance with mankind.

All we want to know in America is simply this: who is for independence, and who is not? Those who are for it, will support it, and the remainder will undoubtedly see the reasonableness of paying the charges; while those who oppose or seek to betray it, must expect the more rigid fate of the jail and the gibbet. There is a bastard kind of generosity, which being extended to all men, is as fatal to society, on one hand, as the want of true generosity is on the other. A lax manner of administering justice, falsely termed moderation, has a tendency both to dispirit public virtue, and promote the growth of public evils. Had the late committee of safety taken cognizance of the last Testimony of the Quakers and proceeded against such delinquents as were concerned therein, they had, probably, prevented the treasonable plans which have been concerted since. When one villain is suffered to escape, it encourages another to proceed, either from a hope of escaping likewise, or an apprehension that we dare not punish. It has been a matter of general surprise, that no notice was taken of the incendiary publication of the Quakers, of the 20th of November last: a publication evidently intended to promote sedition and treason, and encourage the enemy, who were then within a day's march of this city, to proceed on and possess it. I here present the reader with a memorial which was laid before the board of safety a few days after the Testimony appeared. Not a member of that board, that I conversed with, but expressed the highest detestation of the perverted principles and conduct of the Quaker junto, and a wish that the board would take the matter up; notwithstanding which, it was suffered to pass away unnoticed, to the encouragement of new acts of treason, the general danger of the cause, and the disgrace of the state.

To the Honorable the Council of Safety of the State of Pennsylvania

At a meeting of a reputable number of the inhabitants of the city of Philadelphia, impressed with a proper sense of the justice of the cause which this continent is engaged in, and animated with a generous fervor for supporting the same, it was resolved, that the following be laid before the board of safety:

"We profess liberality of sentiment to all men, with this distinction *only*, that those who do not deserve it would become wise and *seek* to deserve it. We hold the pure doctrines of universal liberty of conscience, and conceive it our duty to endeavor to secure that sacred right to others, as well as to defend it for ourselves; for we undertake not to judge of the religious rectitude of tenets, but leave the whole matter to Him who made us.

"We persecute no man, neither will we abet in the persecution of any man for religion's sake; our common relation to others being that of fellow-citizens and fellow subjects of one single community; and in this line of connection we hold out the right hand of fellowship to all men. But we should conceive ourselves to be unworthy members of the *free and independent states of America*, were we unconcernedly to see or to suffer any treasonable wound, public or private, directly or indirectly, to be given against the peace and safety of the same. We inquire not into the rank of the offenders, nor into their religious persuasion; we have no business with either,our part being only to find them out and exhibit them to justice.

"A printed paper, dated the 20th of November, and signed *'John Pemberton,'* whom we suppose to be an inhabitant of this city, has lately been dispersed abroad, a copy of which accompanies this. Had the framers and publishers of that paper conceived it their duty to exhort the youth and others of their society, to a patient submission under the present trying visitations, and humbly to wait the event of heaven towards them, they had therein shown a Christian temper, and we had been silent; but the anger and political virulence with which their instructions are given, and the abuse with which they stigmatize all ranks of men, not thinking like themselves, leave no doubt on our minds from what spirit their publication proceeded: and it is disgraceful to the pure cause of truth, that men can dally with words of the most sacred import, and play them off as mechanically as if religion consisted only in contrivance. We know of no instance in which the Quakers have been compelled to bear arms, or to do any thing which might strain their conscience; wherefore their advice, 'to withstand

and refuse to submit to the arbitrary instructions and ordinances of men,' appear to us a false alarm, and could only be treasonably calculated to gain favor with our enemies, when they are seemingly on the brink of invading this state, or, what is still worse, to weaken the hands of our defence, that their entrance into this city might be made practicable and easy.

"We disclaim all tumult and disorder in the punishment of offenders; and wish to be governed, not by temper but by reason, in the manner of treating them. We are sensible that our cause has suffered by the two following errors; *first*, by ill-judged lenity to traitorous persons in some cases; and, *secondly*, by only a passionate treatment of them in others. For the future we disown both, and wish to be steady in our proceedings, and serious in our punishments.

"Every state in America has, by the repeated voice of its inhabitants, directed and authorized the continental congress to publish a formal declaration of independence of, and separation from, the oppressive king and parliament of Great Britain; and we look on every man as an enemy, who does not in some line or other, give his assistance towards supporting the same; at the same time we consider the offence to be heightened to a degree of unpardonable guilt, when such persons, under the show of religion, endeavor, either by writing, speaking, or otherwise, to subvert, overturn, or bring reproach upon the independence of this continent as declared by congress.

"The publishers of the paper signed 'John Pemberton,' have called in a loud manner to their friends and connections, 'to withstand or refuse' obedience to whatever 'instructions or ordinances' may be published, not warranted by (what they call) 'that happy constitution under which they and others long enjoyed tranquillity and peace.' If this be not treason, we know not what may properly be called by that name.

"To us it is a matter of surprise and astonishment, that men with the word '*Peace, peace,*' continually on their lips, should be so fond of living under and supporting a government, and at the same time calling it '*happy,*' which is never better pleased than when at war—that hath filled India with carnage and famine, Africa with slavery, and tampered with Indians and Negroes to cut the throats of the freemen of America. We conceive it a disgrace to this state, to harbor or wink at such palpable hypocrisy. But as we seek not to hurt the hair of any man's head, when we can make ourselves safe without, we wish such persons to restore peace to themselves and us, by removing themselves to some part of the king of Great Britain's dominions, as by that means they may live unmolested by us and we by them; for our fixed opinion is, that those who do not deserve a place among us, ought not to have one.

"We conclude with requesting the council of safety to take into consideration the paper signed 'John Pemberton,' and if it shall appear to them to be of a dangerous tendency, or of a treasonable nature, that they would commit the signer, together with such other persons as they can discover were concerned therein, into custody, until such time as some mode of trial shall ascertain the full degree of their guilt and punishment: in the doing of which, we wish their judges, whoever they may be, to disregard the man, his connections, interest, riches, poverty, or principles of religion, and to attend to the nature of his offence only."

The most cavilling sectarian cannot accuse the foregoing with containing the least ingredient of persecution. The free spirit on which the American cause is founded, disdains to mix with such an impurity, and leaves it as rubbish fit only for narrow and suspicious minds to grovel in. Suspicion and persecution are weeds of the same dunghill, and flourish together. Had the Quakers minded their religion and their business, they might have lived through this dispute in enviable ease, and none would have molested them. The common phrase with these people is, *'Our principles are peace.'* To which maybe replied, *and your practices are the reverse*; for never did the conduct of men oppose their own doctrine more notoriously than the present race of the Quakers. They have artfully changed themselves into a different sort of people to what they used to be, and yet have the address to persuade each other that they are not altered; like antiquated virgins, they see not the havoc deformity has made upon them, but pleasantly mistaking wrinkles for dimples, conceive themselves yet lovely and wonder at the stupid world for not admiring them.

Did no injury arise to the public by this apostacy of the Quakers from themselves, the public would have nothing to do with it; but as both the design and consequences are pointed against a cause in which the whole community are interested, it is therefore no longer a subject confined, to the cognizance of the meeting only, but comes, as a matter of criminality, before either the authority of the particular state *in which* it is acted, or of the continent *against which* it operates. Every attempt, now, to support the authority of the king and parliament of Great Britain over America is treason against *every* state; therefore it is impossible that any *one* can pardon or screen from punishment an offender against *all*.

But to proceed: while the infatuated tories of this and other states were last spring talking of commissioners, accommodation, making the matter up, and the Lord knows what stuff and nonsense, their *good* king and ministry were glutting themselves with the revenge of reducing America to *unconditional submission*, and solacing each other with the certainty of conquering it in *one campaign*. The following quotations are from the parliamentary register of the debates of the house of lords, March 5th, 1776:

"The Americans," says Lord Talbot,* "have been obstinate, undutiful, and ungovernable from the very beginning, from their first early and infant settlements; and I am every day more and more convinced that this people never will be brought back to their duty, and the subordinate relation they stand in to this country, till *reduced to unconditional, effectual submission; no concession on our part, no lenity, no endurance*, will have any other effect but that of increasing their insolence."

"The struggle," says Lord Townsend,† "is now a struggle for power; the die is cast, and the *only point* which now remains to be determined, is in what manner the war can be most effectually prosecuted and speedily finished, in order to procure that *unconditional submission*, which has been so ably stated by the noble earl with the white staff;" (meaning Lord Talbot,) "and I have no reason to doubt that the measures now pursuing will put an end to the war in the course of a *single campaign*. Should it linger longer, we shall then have reason to expect that some foreign power will interfere, and take advantage of our domestic troubles and civil distractions."

Lord Littleton. "My sentiments are pretty well known. I shall only observe now that lenient measures have had no other effect than to produce insult after insult; that the more we conceded, the higher America rose in her demands, and the more insolent she has grown. It is for this reason that I am now for the most effective and decisive measures; and am of opinion that no alternative is left us, but to relinquish America for ever,

---

*Steward, of the king's household.

†Formerly, General Townsend, at Quebec, and late lord-lieutenant of Ireland.

or finally determine to compel her to acknowledge the legislative authority of this country; and it is the principle of an *unconditional submission* I would be for maintaining."

Can words be more expressive than these? Surely the tories will believe the tory lords! The truth is, they *do believe them* and know as fully as any whig on the continent knows, that the king and ministry never had the least design of an accommodation with America, but an absolute, unconditional conquest. And the part which the tories were to act, was, by downright lying, to endeavor to put the continent off its guard, and to divide and sow discontent in the minds of such whigs as they might gain and influence over. In short, to keep up a distraction here, that the force sent from England might be able to conquer in *"one campaign."* They and the ministry were, by a different game, playing into each others hands. The cry of the tories in England was, *"No reconciliation, no accommodation,"* in order to obtain the greater military force; while those in America were crying nothing but *"reconciliation and accommodation,"* that the force sent might conquer with the less resistance.

But this *"single campaign"* is over, and America not conquered. The whole work is yet to do, and the force much less to do it with. Their condition is both despicable and deplorable: Out of cash—out of heart, and out of hope. A country furnished with arms and ammunition, as America now is, with three millions of inhabitants, and three thousand miles distant from the nearest enemy that can approach her, is able to look and laugh them in the face.

Howe appears to have two objects in view, either to go up the North River, or come to Philadelphia.

By going up the North River, he secures a retreat for his army through Canada, but the ships must return if they return at all, the same way they went; and as our army would be in the rear, the safety of their passage down is a doubtful matter. By such a motion he shuts himself from all supplies from Europe, but through Canada, and exposes his army and navy to the danger of perishing. The idea of his cutting off the communication between the eastern and southern states, by means of the North River, is merely visionary. He cannot do it by his shipping; because no ship can lay long at anchor in any river within reach of the shore; a single gun would drive a first rate vessel from such a station. This was fully proved last October at forts Washington and Lee, where one gun only, on each side of the river, obliged two frigates to cut and be towed off in an hour's time. Neither can he cut it off by his army: because the several posts they must occupy, would divide them almost to nothing, and expose them to be picked up by ours like pebbles on a river's bank; but admitting that he could, where is the injury? Because, while his whole force is cantoned out, as sentries over the water, they will be very innocently employed, and the moment they march into the country, the communication opens.

The most probable object is Philadelphia, and the reasons are many. Howe's business in America is to conquer it, and in proportion as he finds himself unable to the task, he will employ his strength to distress women and weak minds, in order to effect through *their* fears what he cannot accomplish by his *own* force. His coming or attempting to come to Philadelphia is a circumstance that proves his weakness: for no general that felt himself able to take the field and attack his antagonist, would think of bringing his army into a city in the summer time; and this mere shifting the scene from place to place, without effecting any thing, has feebleness and cowardice on the face of it, and holds him up in a contemptible light to all who can reason justly and firmly. By several informations from New York, it appears that their army in general, both officers and men, have given up the expectation of conquering America; their eye now is fixed upon the spoil. They suppose Philadelphia to be rich with stores, and as they think to get more by robbing a town than by attacking an army, their movement towards this city is probable. We are not now contending against an army of soldiers, but against a band of thieves, who had rather plunder than fight, and have no other hope of conquest than by cruelty.

They expect to get a mighty booty, and strike another general panic, by making a sudden movement and getting possession of this city; but unless they can march *out* as well as *in*, or get the entire command of the river, to remove off their plunder, they may probably be stopped with the stolen goods upon them. They have never yet succeeded wherever they have been opposed, but at Fort Washington. At Charleston their defeat was effectual. At Ticonderoga they ran away. In every skirmish at Kingsbridge and the White Plains they were obliged to retreat, and the instant our arms were turned upon them in the Jerseys, they turned likewise, and those that turned not were taken.

The necessity of always fitting our internal police to the circumstances of the times we live in, is something so strikingly obvious, that no sufficient objection can be made against it. The safety of all societies depends upon it; and where this point is not attended to, the consequences will either be a general languor or a tumult. The encouragement and protection of the good subjects of any state, and the suppression and punishment of bad ones, are the principal objects for which all authority is instituted, and the line in which it ought to operate. We have in this city a strange variety of men and characters, and the circumstances of the times require that they should be publicly known; it is not the number of tories that hurt us, so much as the not finding out who they are; men must now take one side or the other, and abide by the consequences: the Quakers, trusting to their short-sighted sagacity, have, most unluckily for them, made their declaration in their last Testimony, and we ought *now* to take them at their word. They have voluntarily read themselves out of the continental meeting, and cannot hope to be restored to it again but by payment and penitence. Men whose political principles are founded on avarice, are beyond the reach of reason, and the only cure of toryism of this cast, is to tax it. A substantial good drawn from a real evil, is of the same benefit to society, as if drawn from a virtue; and where men have not public spirit to render themselves serviceable, it ought to be the study of government to draw the best use possible from their vices. When the governing passion of any man, or set of men, is once known, the method of managing them is easy; for even misers, whom no public virtue can impress, would become generous, could a heavy tax be laid upon covetousness.

The tories have endeavored to insure their property with the enemy, by forfeiting their reputation with us; from which may be justly inferred, that their governing passion is avarice. Make them as much afraid of losing on one side as on the other, and you stagger their toryism; make them more so, and you reclaim them; for their principle is to worship any power they are most afraid of.

This method of considering men and things together, opens into a large field for speculation, and affords me an opportunity of offering some observations on the state of our currency, so as to make the support of it go hand in hand with the suppression of disaffection and the encouragement of public spirit.

The thing which first presents itself in inspecting the state of the currency, is, that we have too much of it, and that there is a necessity of reducing the quantity, in order to increase the value. Men are daily growing poor by the very means they take to get rich; for in the same proportion that the prices of all goods on hand are raised, the value of all money laid by is reduced. A simple case will make this clear; let a man have £100, in cash, and as many goods on hand as will to-day sell for £20, but not content with the present market price, he raises them to £40, and by so doing obliges others, in their own defence, to raise cent. per cent. likewise; in this case it is evident that his hundred pounds laid by, is reduced fifty pounds in value; whereas, had the market lowered cent. per cent. his goods would have sold but for ten, but his hundred pounds would have risen in value to two hundred; because it would then purchase as many goods again, or support his family as long again as before. And, strange as it may seem, he is one hundred and fifty pounds the poorer for raising his goods, to what he would have been had he lowered them; because the forty pounds which his goods sold for, is, by the general rise of the markets cent. per cent., rendered of no more value than the ten pounds would be had the markeT fallen in the same proportion; and, consequently, the whole difference of gain or loss is on the difference in value of the hundred pounds laid by, *viz.* from fifty to two hundred. This rage for raising goods is for several reasons much more the fault of the tories than the whigs; and yet the tories (to their shame and confusion ought they to be told of it) are by far the most noisy and discontented. The greatest part of the whigs, by being now either in the army or employed in some public service, are *buyers* only and not *sellers*, and as this evil has its origin in trade, it cannot be charged on those who are out of it.

But the grievance has now become too general to be remedied by partial methods, and the only effectual cure is to reduce the quantity of money: With half the quantity we should be richer than we are now, because the value of it would be doubled, and consequently our attachment to it increased; for it is not the number of dollars a man has, but how far they will go, that makes him either rich or poor.

These two points being admitted, *viz*. that the quantity of money is too great, and that the prices of goods can be only effectually reduced by reducing the quantity of the money, the next point to be considered is, the method how to reduce it.

The circumstances of the times, as before observed, require that the public characters of all men should *now* be fully understood, and the only general method of ascertaining it is by an oath or affirmation, renouncing all allegiance to the king of Great Britain, and to support the independence of the United States as declared by congress. Let, at the same time, a tax of ten, fifteen or twenty per cent. per annum, to be collected quarterly, be levied on all property. These alternatives, by being perfectly voluntary, will take in all sorts of people. Here is the test; here is the tax. He who takes the former, conscientiously proves his affection to the cause, and binds himself to pay his quota by the best *services* in his power, and is thereby justly exempt from the latter; and those who choose the latter, pay their quota in money, to be excused from taking the former, or rather 'tis the price paid to us for their supposed, though mistaken, insurance with the enemy.

But this is only a part of the advantage which would arise by knowing the different characters of men. The whigs stake every thing on the issue of their arms, while the tories, by their disaffection, are sapping and undermining their strength; and, of consequence, the property of the whigs is the more exposed thereby; and whatever injury their estates may sustain by the movements of the enemy, must either be borne by themselves, who have done every thing which has *yet* been done, or by the tories, who have not only done nothing, but have by their disaffection, invited the enemy on.

In the present crisis we ought to know square by square, and house by house, who are in real allegiance with the United Independent States, and who are not. Let but the line be made clear and distinct, and all men will then know what they are to trust to. It would not only be good policy, but strict justice, to raise fifty or a hundred thousand pounds, or more, if it is necessary, out of the estates and property of the king of England's votaries, resident in Philadelphia, to be distributed, as a reward to those inhabitants of the city and state, who should turn out and repulse the enemy, should they attempt their march this way; and likewise, to bind the property of all such persons to make good the damages which that of the whigs might sustain. In the undistinguishable mode of conducting a war, we frequently make reprisals at sea on the vessels of persons in England, who are friends to our cause compared with the resident tories among us.

In every former publication of mine, from *Common Sense* down to the last *Crisis*, I have generally gone on the charitable supposition, that the tories were rather a mistaken than a criminal people, and have applied argument after argument with all the candor and temper I was capable of, in order to set every part of the case clearly and fairly before them, and if possible to reclaim them from ruin to reason. I have done my duty by them and have now done with that doctrine, taking it for granted, that those who yet hold their disaffection, are, either a set of avaricious miscreants, who would sacrifice the continent to save themselves, or a banditti of hungry traitors, who are hoping for a division of the spoil. To which may be added, a list of crown or proprietary. dependants, who, rather than go without a portion of power, would be content to share it with the devil. Of such men there is no hope; and their obedience will only be according to the danger that is set before them, and the power that is exercised over them.

A time will shortly arrive, in which, by ascertaining the characters of persons now, we shall be guarded against their mischiefs then; for in proportion as the enemy despair of conquest, they will be trying the arts of seduction and the force of fear by all the mischiefs they can inflict. But in war we may be certain of these two things, *viz.* that cruelty in an enemy, and motions made with more than usual parade, are always signs of weakness. He that can conquer, finds his mind too free and pleasant to be brutish; and he that intends to conquer, never makes too much show of his strength.

We now know the enemy we have to do with. While drunk with the certainty of victory, they disdained to be civil; and in proportion as disappointment makes them sober, and their apprehensions of an European war alarm them, they will become cringing and artful; honest they cannot be. But our answer to them, in either condition they may be in, is short and full,—"As free and independent states we are willing to make peace with you to-morrow, but we can neither hear nor reply in any other character."

If Britain cannot conquer us, it proves, that she is neither able to govern nor protect us, and our particular situation now is such, that any connection with her would be unwisely exchanging a half-defeated enemy for two powerful ones. Europe, by every appearance and information, is now on the eve, nay, on the morning twilight of a war, and any alliance with *George the third* brings *France* and *Spain* upon our backs;

a separation from him attaches them to our side; therefore, the only road to *peace*, *honor* and commerce, is *Independence*.

Written this fourth year of the UNION, *which God preserve.*

COMMON SENSE.
Philadelphia, April 19, 1777.

THE CRISIS
NUMBER IV

THOSE who expect to reap the blessings of freedom, must, like men, undergo the fatigues of supporting it. The event of yesterday was one of those kind alarms which is just sufficient to rouse us to duty, without being of consequence enough to depress our fortitude. It is not a field of a few acres of ground, but a cause, that we are defending, and whether we defeat the enemy in one battle, or by degrees, the consequence will be the same.

Look back at the events of last winter and the present year, there you will find that the enemy's successes always contributed to reduce them. What they have gained in ground, they paid so dearly for in numbers, that their victories have in the end amounted to defeats. We have always been masters at the last push, and always shall be while we do our duty. Howe has been once on the banks of the Delaware, and from thence driven back with loss and disgrace: and why not be again driven from the Schuylkill? His condition and ours are very different. He has every body to fight, we have only his *one* army to cope with, and which wastes away at every engagement: we can not only reinforce, but can redouble our numbers; he is cut off from all supplies, and must sooner or later inevitably fall into our hands.

Shall a band of ten or twelve thousand robbers, who are this day fifteen hundred or two thousand men less in strength than they were yesterday, conquer America, or subdue even a single state? The thing cannot be, unless we sit down and suffer them to do it. Another such a brush, notwithstanding we lost the ground, would, by still reducing the enemy, put them in a condition to be afterwards totally defeated.

Could our whole army have come up to the attack at one time, the consequences had probably been otherwise; but our having different parts of the Brandywine Creek to guard, and the uncertainty which road to Philadelphia the enemy would attempt to take, naturally afforded them an opportunity of passing with their main body to a place where only a part of ours could be posted; for it must strike every thinking man with conviction, that it requires a much greater force to oppose an enemy in several places, than is sufficient to defeat him in any one place.

Men who are sincere in defending their freedom, will always feel concern at every circumstance which seems to make against them; it is the natural and honest consequence of all affectionate attachments, and the want of it is a vice. But the dejection lasts only for a moment; they soon rise out of it with additional vigor; the glow of hope, courage and fortitude, will, in a little time, supply the place of every inferior passion, and kindle the whole heart into heroism.

There is a mystery in the countenance of some causes, which we have not always present judgment enough to explain. It is distressing to see an enemy advancing into a country, but it is the only place in which we can beat them, and in which we have always beaten them, whenever they made the attempt. The nearer any disease approaches to a crisis, the nearer it is to a cure. Danger and deliverance make their advances together, and it is only the last push, that one or the other takes the lead.

There are many men who will do their duty when it is not wanted; but a genuine public spirit always appears most when there is most occasion for it. Thank God! our army, though fatigued, is yet entire. The attack made by us yesterday, was under many disadvantages, naturally arising from the uncertainty of knowing which route the enemy would take; and, from that circumstance, the whole of our force could not be brought up together time enough to engage all at once. Our strength is yet reserved; and it is evident that Howe does not think himself a gainer by the affair, otherwise he would this morning have moved down and attacked General Washington.

Gentlemen of the city and country, it is in your power, by a spirited improvement of the present circumstance, to turn it to a real advantage. Howe is now weaker than before, and every shot will contribute to reduce him. You are more immediately interested than any other part of the continent; your all is at stake; it is not so with the general cause; you are devoted by the enemy to plunder and destruction: it is the encouragement which Howe, the chief of plunderers, has promised his army. Thus circumstanced, you may save yourselves by a manly resistance, but can have no hope in any other conduct. I never yet knew our brave general, or any part of the army, officers or men, out of heart, and I have seen them in circumstances a thousand times more trying than the present. It is only those that are not in action, that feel languor and heaviness, and the best way to rub it off is to turn out, and make sure work of it.

Our army must undoubtedly feel fatigue, and want a reinforcement of rest, though not of valor. Our own interest and happiness call upon us to give them every support in our power, and make the burden of the day, on which the safety of this city depends, as light as possible. Remember, gentlemen, that we have forces both to the northward and southward of Philadelphia, and if the enemy be but stopped till those can arrive, this city will be saved, and the enemy finally routed.

You have too much at stake to hesitate. You ought not to think an hour upon the matter, but to spring to action at once. Other states have been invaded, have likewise driven off the invaders. Now our time and turn is come, and perhaps the finishing stroke is reserved for us. When we look back on the dangers we have been saved from, and reflect on the success we have been blessed with, it would be sinful either to be idle or to despair.

I close this paper with a short address to General Howe. You, sir, are only lingering out the period that shall bring with it your defeat. You have yet scarce began upon the war, and the further you enter, the faster will your troubles thicken. What you now enjoy is only a respite from ruin; an invitation to destruction; something that will lead on to our deliverance at your expense. We know the cause which we are engaged in, and though a passionate fondness for it may make us grieve at every injury which threatens it, when the moment of concern is over, the determination to duty returns. We are not moved by the gloomy smile of a worthless king, but by the ardent glow of generous patriotism. We fight not to enslave, but to set a country free, and to make room upon the earth for honest men to live in. In such a cause we are sure that we are right; and we leave to you the despairing reflection of being the tool of a miserable tyrant.

COMMON SENSE.
Philadelphia, Sept. 12, 1777.

THE CRISIS
NUMBER V

To General Sir William Howe

TO argue with a man who has renounced the use and authority of reason, and whose philosophy consists in holding humanity in contempt, is like administering medicine to the dead, or endeavoring to convert an atheist by scripture. Enjoy, sir, your insensibility of feeling and reflecting.—It is the prerogative of animals. And no man will envy you those honors, in which a savage only can be your rival, and a bear your master.

As the generosity of this country rewarded your brother's services last war, with an elegant monument in Westminster Abbey, it is consistent that she should bestow some mark of distinction upon you. You certainly deserve her notice, and a conspicuous place in the catalogue of extraordinary persons. Yet it would be a pity to pass you from the world in state, and consign you to magnificent oblivion among the tombs, without telling the future beholder why. Judas is as much known as John, yet history ascribes their fame to very different actions.

Sir William hath undoubtedly merited a monument: but of what kind, or with what inscription, where placed or how embellished, is a question that would puzzle all the heralds of St. James's in the profoundest mood of historical deliberation. We are at no loss, sir, to ascertain your real character, but somewhat perplexed how to perpetuate its identity, and preserve it uninjured from the transformations of time or mistake. A statuary may give a false expression to your bust, or decorate it with some equivocal emblems, by which you may happen to steal into reputation and impose upon the hereafter traditionary world. Ill nature or ridicule may conspire, or a variety of accidents combine to lessen, enlarge, or change Sir William's fame; and no doubt but he who has taken so much pains to be singular in his conduct, would choose to be just as singular in his exit, his monument, and his epitaph.

The usual honors of the dead, to be sure, are not sufficiently sublime, to escort a character like you to the republic of dust and ashes; for however men may differ in their ideas of grandeur or of government here, the grave is nevertheless a perfect republic. Death is not the monarch of the dead, but of the dying. The moment he obtains a conquest he loses a subject, and, like the foolish king you serve, will, in the end, war himself out all his dominions.

As a proper preliminary towards the arrangement of your funeral honors, we readily admit your new rank of *knighthood*. The title is perfectly in character, and is your own, more by merit than creation. There are knights of various orders, from the knight of the windmill to the knight of the post. The former is your patron for exploits, and the latter will assist you in settling your accounts. No honorary title could be more happily applied! The ingenuity is sublime! And your royal master hath discovered more genius in fitting you therewith, than in generating the most finished figure for a button, or descanting on the properties of a button mould.

But how, sir, shall we dispose of you? The invention of a statuary is exhausted, and Sir William is yet unprovided with a monument. America is anxious to bestow her funeral favors upon you, and wishes to do it in a manner that shall distinguish you from all the deceased heroes of the last war. The *Egyptian method of embalming* is not known to the present age, and hieroglyphical pageantry hath outlived the science of deciphering it. Some other method, therefore, must be, thought of to immortalize the new knight of the windmill and post. Sir William, thanks to his stars, is not oppressed with very delicate ideas. He has no ambition of being wrapped up and handled about in myrrh, aloes and cassia. Less expensive odors will suffice; and it fortunately happens, that the simple genius of America hath discovered the art of preserving bodies, and embellishing them too, with much greater frugality than the ancients. In a balmage, sir, of humble tar, you will be as secure as Pharaoh, and in a hieroglyphic of feathers, rival in finery all the mummies of Egypt.

As you have already made your exit from the moral world, and by numberless acts both of passionate and deliberate injustice engraved an *"here lyeth"* on your deceased honor, it must be mere affectation in you to pretend concern at the humors or opinions of mankind respecting you. What remains of you may expire at any time. The sooner the better. For he who survives his reputation, lives out of despite of himself, like a man listening to his own reproach.

Thus entombed and ornamented, I leave you to the inspection of the curious, and return to the history of your yet surviving actions.—The character of Sir William hath undergone some extraordinary revolutions since his arrival in America. It is now fixed and known; and we have nothing to hope from your candor or to fear from your capacity. Indolence and inability have too large a share in your composition, ever to suffer you to be any thing more than the hero of little villainies and unfinished adventures. That, which to some persons appeared moderation in you at first, was not produced by any real virtue of your own, but by a contrast of passions, dividing and holding you in perpetual irreolution. One vice will frequently expel another, without the least merit in the man; as powers in contrary directions reduce each other to rest.

It became you to have supported a dignified solemnity of character; to have shown a superior liberality of soul; to have won respect by an obstinate perseverance in maintaining order, and to have exhibited on all occasions, such an unchangeable graciousness of conduct, that while we beheld in you the resolution of an enemy, we might admire in you the sincerity of a man. You came to America under the high-sounding titles of commander and commissioner; not only to suppress what you call rebellion by arms, but to shame it out of countenance by the excellence of your example. Instead of which, you have been the patron of low and vulgar frauds, the encourager of Indian cruelties; and have imported a cargo of vices blacker than those you pretended to suppress.

Mankind are not universally agreed in their determination of right and wrong; but there are certain actions which the consent of all nations and individuals hath branded with the unchangeable name of *meanness*. In the list of human vices we find some of such a refined constitution, that they cannot be carried into practice without seducing some virtue to their assistance; but *meanness* hath neither alliance nor apology. It is generated in the dust and sweepings of other vices, and is of such a hateful figure that all the rest conspire to disown it. Sir William, the commissioner of George the Third, hath at last vouchsafed to give it rank and pedigree. He has placed the fugitive at the council board, and dubbed it companion of the order of knighthood.

The particular act of meanness which I allude to in this description, is forgery. You, sir, have abetted and patronized the forging and uttering counterfeit continental bills. In the same New York newspapers in which your own proclamation under your masters authority was published, offering, or pretending to offer, pardon and protection to the inhabitants of these states, there were repeated advertisements of counterfeit money for sale, and persons who have come officially from you, and under the sanction of your flag, have been taken up in attempting to put them off.

A conduct so basely mean in a public character is without precedent or pretence. Every nation on earth, whether friends or enemies, will unite in despising you. 'Tis an incendiary war upon society, which nothing can excuse or palliate.—An improvement upon beggarly villainy—and shows an inbred wretchedness of heart made up between the venomous malignity of a serpent and the spiteful imbecility of an inferior reptile.

The laws of any civilized country would condemn you to the gibbet without regard to your rank or titles, because it is an action foreign to the usage and custom of war; and should you fall into our hands, which pray God you may, it will be a doubtful matter whether we are to consider you as a military prisoner or a prisoner for felony.

Besides, it is exceedingly unwise and impolitic in you, or any persons in the English service, to promote or even encourage, or wink at the crime of forgery, in any case whatever. Because, as the riches of England, as a nation, are chiefly in paper, and the far greater part of trade among individuals is carried on by the same medium, that is, by notes and drafts on one another, they, therefore, of all people in the world, ought to endeavor to keep forgery out of sight, and, if possible, not to revive the idea of it. It is dangerous to make men familiar with a crime which they may afterwards practice to much greater advantage against those who first taught them. Several officers in the English army have made their exit at the gallows for forgery on their agents; for we all know, who know any thing of England, that there is not a more necessitous body of men, taking them generally, than what the English officers are. They contrive to make a show at the expense of the tailors, and appear clean at the charge of the washer-women.

England, hath at this time, nearly two hundred million pounds sterling of public money in paper, for which she hath no real property: besides a large circulation of bank notes, bank post bills, and promissory notes and drafts of private bankers, merchants and tradesmen. She hath the greatest quantity of paper currency and the least quantity of gold and silver of any nation in Europe; the real specie which is about sixteen millions sterling, serves only as change in large sums, which are always made in paper, or for payment in small ones. Thus circumstanced, the nation is put to its wit's end, and obliged to be severe almost to criminality, to prevent the practice and growth of forgery. Scarcely a session passes at the Old Bailly, or an execution at Tyburn, but witnesseth this truth. Yet you, sir, regardless of the policy which her necessity obliges her to adopt, have made your whole army intimate with the crime. And as all armies, at the conclusion of a war, are too apt to carry into practice the vices of the campaign, it will probably happen, that England will hereafter abound in forgeries, to which art, the practitioners were first initiated under your authority in America. You, sir, have the honor of adding a new vice to the military catalogue; and the reason, perhaps, why the invention was reserved for you, is, because no general before was mean enough even to think of it.

That a man whose soul is absorbed in the low traffic of vulgar vice, is incapable of moving in any superior region, is clearly shown in you by the event of every campaign. Your military exploits have been without plan, object or decision.

Can it be possible that you or your employers suppose that the possession of Philadelphia will be any ways equal to the expense or expectation of the nation which supports you? What advantages does England derive from any achievements of yours? To *her* it is perfectly indifferent what place you are in, so long as the business of conquest is unperformed and the charge of maintaining you remains the same.

If the principal events of the three campaigns be attended to, the balance will appear strongly against you at the close of each; but the last, in point of importance to us, has exceeded the former two. It is pleasant to look back on dangers past, and equally as pleasant to meditate on present ones when the way out begins to appear. *That* period is now arrived, and the long doubtful winter of war is changing to the sweeter prospects of victory and joy. At the close of the campaign, in 1775, you were obliged to retreat from Boston. In the summer of 1776, you appeared with a numerous fleet and army in the harbor of New York. By what miracle the continent was preserved in that season of danger is a subject of admiration! If instead of wasting your time against Long Island, you had run up the North River, and landed any where above New York, the consequence must have been, that either you would have compelled General Washington to fight you with very unequal numbers, or he must have suddenly evacuated the city with the loss of nearly all the stores of the army, or have surrendered for want of provisions: the situation of the place naturally producing one or the other of these events.

The preparations made to defend New York were, nevertheless, wise and military; because your forces were then at sea, their number uncertain: storms, sickness, or a variety of accidents might have disabled their coming, or so diminished them on their passage, that those which survived would have been incapable of opening the campaign with any prospect of success; in which case the defence would have been sufficient and the place preserved: for cities that have been raised from nothing with an infinitude of labor and expense, are not to be thrown away on the bare probability of their being taken. On these grounds the preparations made to maintain New York were as judicious as the retreat afterwards. While you, in the interim, let slip the *very* opportunity which seemed to put conquest in your power.

Through the whole of that campaign you had nearly double the forces which General Washington immediately commanded. The principal plan at that time, on our part, was to wear away the season with as little loss as possible, and to raise the army for the next year. Long Island, New York, Forts Washington and Lee were not defended after your superior force was known, under any expectation of their being finally maintained, but as a range of outworks, in the attacking of which your time might be wasted, your numbers reduced, and your vanity amused by possessing them on our retreat. It was intended to have withdrawn the garrison from Fort Washington after it had answered the former of those purposes, but the fate of that day put a prize into your hands without much honor to yourselves.

Your progress through the Jerseys was accidental; you had it not even in contemplation, or you would not have sent a principal part of your forces to Rhode Island before hand. The utmost hope of America in the year 1776, reached no higher than that she might not then be conquered. She had no expectation of defeating you in that campaign. Even the most cowardly tory allowed, that, could she withstand the shock of *that* summer her independence would be past a doubt. You had *then* greatly the advantage of her. You were formidable. Your military knowledge was supposed to be complete. Your fleets and forces arrived without an accident. You had neither experience nor reinforcements to wait for. You had nothing to do but to begin, and your chance lay in the first vigorous onset.

America was young and unskilled. She was obliged to trust her defence to time and practice; and hath, by mere dint of perseverance, maintained her cause, and brought her enemy to a condition in which she is now capable of meeting him on any grounds.

It is remarkable that in the campaign of seventy-six, you gained no more, notwithstanding your great force, than what was given you by consent of evacuation, except Fort Washington: while every advantage obtained by us was by fair and hard fighting. The defeat of Sir Peter Parker was complete. The conquest of the Hessians at Trenton by the remains of a retreating army, which but a few days before you affected to despise, is an instance of heroic perseverance very seldom to be met with. And the victory over the British troops at Princeton, by a harassed and wearied party, who had been engaged the day before and marched all night without refreshment, is attended with such a scene of circumstances and superiority of generalship, as will ever give it a place on the first line in the history of great actions.

When I look back on the gloomy days of last winter and see America suspended by a thread, I feel a triumph of joy at the recollection of her delivery, and a reverence for the characters which snatched her from destruction. To doubt *now* would be a species of infidelity, and to forget the instruments which saved us *then* would be ingratitude.

The close of that campaign left us with the spirit of conquerors. The northern districts were relieved by the retreat of General Carleton over the lakes. The army under your command were hunted back and had their bounds prescribed. The continent began to feel its military importance, and the winter passed pleasantly away in preparations for the next campaign.

However confident you might be on your first arrival, the course of the year seventy-six gave you some idea of the difficulty, if not impossibility, of conquest. To this reason I ascribe your delay in opening the campaign of seventy-seven. The face of matters, on the close of the former year, gave you no encouragement to pursue a discretionary war as soon as the spring admitted the taking the field: for though conquest, in that case, would have given you a double portion of fame, yet the experiment was too hazardous. The ministry, had you failed, would have shifted the whole blame upon you, charged you with having acted without orders, and condemned at once both your plan and your execution.

To avoid those misfortunes, which might have involved you and your money accounts in perplexity and suspicion, you prudently waited the arrival of a plan of operations from England, which was, that you should proceed for Philadelphia by the way of the Chesapeake, and that Burgoyne, after reducing Ticonderoga, should take his route by Albany, and, if necessary, join you.

The splendid laurels of the last campaign have flourished in the north. In that quarter America hath surprised the world, and laid the foundation of her this year's glory. The conquest of Ticonderoga (if it may be called a conquest) has, like all your other victories, led on to ruin. Even the provisions taken in that fortress (which by General Burgoyne's return was sufficient in bread and flour for nearly 5,000 men for ten weeks, and in beef and pork for the same number of men for one month) served only to hasten his overthrow, by enabling him to proceed to Saratoga, the place of his destruction. A short review of the operations of the last campaign will show the condition of affairs on both sides.

You have taken Ticonderoga and marched into Philadelphia. These are all the events which the year hath produced on your part. A trifling campaign indeed, compared with the expenses of England and the conquest of the continent. On the other side, a considerable part of your northern force has been routed by the New York militia under General Herkemer; Fort Stanwix hath bravely survived a compound attack of soldiers and savages, and the besiegers have fled. The battle of Bennington has put a thousand prisoners into our hands, with all their arms, stores, artillery and baggage. General Burgoyne in two engagements has been defeated; himself, his army, and all that were his and theirs are now ours. Ticonderoga and Independence are retaken, and not the shadow of an enemy remains in all the northern districts. At this instant we have upwards of eleven thousand prisoners, between sixty and seventy pieces of brass ordinance, besides small arms, tents, stores, &c.

In order to know the real value of those advantages we must reverse the scene, and suppose General Gates and the force be commanded, to be at your mercy as prisoners, and General Burgoyne with his army of soldiers and savages to be already joined to you in Pennsylvania. So dismal a picture can scarcely be looked at. It hath all the tracings and colorings of horror and despair; and excites the most swelling emotions of gratitude by exhibiting the miseries we are so graciously preserved from.

I admire this distribution of laurels around the continent. It is the earnest of future union. South Carolina has had her day of suffering and of fame; and the other southern states have exerted themselves in proportion to the force that invaded or insulted them. Towards the close of the campaign in sev-

enty-six, these middle states were called upon and did their
duty nobly. They were witnesses to the almost expiring flame
of human freedom. It was the close struggle of life and
death,—the line of invisible division; and on which, the
unabated fortitude of a Washington prevailed, and saved the
spark that has since blazed in the north with unrivalled lustre.

Let me ask, sir, what great exploits have you performed?
Through all the variety of changes and opportunities which
this war hath produced, I know no one action of yours that can
be styled masterly. You have moved in and out, backward and
forward, round and round, as if valor consisted in a military
jig. The history and figure of your movements would be truly
ridiculous could they be justly delineated. They resemble the
labors of a puppy pursuing his tail; the end is still at the same
distance, and all the turnings round must be done over again.

The first appearance of affairs at Ticonderoga wore such
an unpromising aspect, that it was necessary, in July, to detach
a part of the forces to the support of that quarter, which were
otherwise destined or intended to act against you, and this, perhaps, has been the means of postponing your downfall to
another campaign. The destruction of one army at a time is
work enough. We know, sir, what we are about, what we have
to do, and how to do it.

Your progress from the Chesapeake was marked by no
capital stroke of policy or heroism. Your principal aim was to
get General Washington between the Delaware and Schuylkill
and between Philadelphia and your army. In that situation,
with a river on each of his flanks, which united about five
miles below the city, and your army above him, you could have
intercepted his reinforcements and supplies, cut off all his
communication, with the country, and, if necessary, have dis-
patched assistance to open a passage for General Burgoyne.

This scheme was too visible to succeed, for had General Washington suffered you to command the open country above him, I think it a very reasonable conjecture that the conquest of Burgoyne would not have taken place because you could, in that case, have relieved him. It was therefore necessary, while that important victory was in suspense, to trepan *you* into a situation, in which you could only be on the defensive, without the power of affording him assistance. The manœuvre had its effect and Burgoyne was conquered.

There has been something unmilitary passive in you from the time of your passing the Schuylkill and getting possession of Philadelphia to the close of the campaign. You mistook a trap for a conquest, the probability of which had been made known to Europe, and the edge of your triumph taken off by our own information long before.

Having got you into this situation, a scheme for a general attack upon you at Germantown was carried into execution on the fourth of October, and though the success was not equal to the excellence of the plan, yet the attempting it proved the genius of America to be on the rise, and her power approaching to superiority. The obscurity of the morning was your best friend, for a fog is always favorable to a hunted enemy. Some weeks after this, you likewise planned an attack on General Washington while at Whitemarsh. Marched out with infinite parade, but on finding him preparing to attack you the next morning, you prudently cut about and retreated to Philadelphia, with all the precipitation of a man conquered in imagination.

Immediately after the battle of Germantown, the probability of Burgoyne's defeat gave a new policy to affairs in Pennsylvania, and it was judged most consistent with the general safety of America to wait the issue of the Northern campaign. Slow and sure is sound work. The news of that victory arrived in our camp on the 18th of October, and no sooner did the shout of joy and the report of the thirteen cannon reach your ears, than you resolved upon a retreat, and the next day, that is on the 19th, withdrew your drooping army into Philadelphia. This movement was evidently dictated by fear; and carried with it a positive confession that you dreaded a second attack. It was hiding yourself among women and children, and sleeping away the choicest part of a campaign in expensive inactivity. An army in a city can never be a conquering army. The situation admits only of defense. It is mere shelter; and every military power in Europe will conclude you to be eventually defeated.

The time when you made this retreat was the very time you ought to have fought a battle, in order to put yourself in a condition of recovering in Pennsylvania what you had lost at Saratoga. And the reason why you did not, must be either prudence or cowardice; the former supposes your inability, and the latter needs no explanation. I draw no conclusions, sir, but such as are naturally deduced from known and visible facts, and such as will always have a being while the facts which produced them remain unaltered.

After this retreat a new difficulty arose which exhibited the power of Britain in a very contemptible light, which was the attack and defence of Mud Island. For several weeks did that little unfinished fortress stand out against all the attempts of Admiral and General Howe. It was the fable of Bendar realized on the Delaware. Scheme after scheme, and force upon force were tried and defeated. The garrison, with scarce any thing to cover them but their bravery, survived in the midst of mud, shot and shells, and were at last obliged to give it up, more to the powers of time and gunpowder than to the military superiority of the besiegers.

It is my sincere opinion that matters are in a much worse

condition with you than what is generally known. Your master's speech at the opening of parliament is like a soliloquy on ill luck. It shows him to be coming a little to his reason, for sense of pain is the first symptom of recovery in profound stupefactions. His condition is deplorable. He is obliged to submit to all the insults of France and Spain, without daring to know or resent them; and thankful for the most trivial evasions to the most humble remonstrances. The time *was* when he could not *deign* an answer to a petition from America, and the time now *is* when he dare not *give* an answer to an affront from France. The capture of Burgoyne's army will sink his consequence as much in Europe as in America. In his speech he expresses his suspicions at the warlike preparations of France and Spain, and as he has only the one army which you command to support his character in the world with, it remains very uncertain when, or in what quarter, it will be most wanted or can be best employed; and this will partly account for the great care you take to keep it from action and attacks, for should Burgoyne's fate be yours, which it probably will, England may take her endless farewell not only of all America but of all the West Indies.

Never did a nation invite destruction upon itself with the eagerness and ignorance with which Britain had done. Bent upon the ruin of a young and unoffending country, she hath drawn the sword that hath wounded herself to the heart, and in the agony of her resentment hath applied a poison for a cure. Her conduct towards America is a compound of rage and lunacy; she aims at the government of it, yet preserves neither dignity nor character in her methods to obtain it. Were government a mere manufacture or article of commerce, immaterial by whom it should be made or sold, we might as well employ her as another, but when we consider it as the fountain from whence the general manners and morality of a country take their rise, that the persons intrusted with the execution thereof are by their serious example and authority to support these principles, how abominably absurd is the idea of being hereafter governed by a set of men who have been guilty of forgery, perjury, treachery, theft, and every species of villainy which the lowest wretches on earth could practice or invent. What greater public curse can befall any country than to be under such authority, and what greater blessing than to be delivered therefrom? The soul of any man of sentiment would rise in brave rebellion against them and spurn them from the earth.

The malignant and venomous tempered General Vaughan has amused his savage fancy in burning the whole town of Kingston, in York government, and the late governor of that state, Mr. Tryon, in his letter to General Parsons, has endeavored to justify it, and declared his wish to burn the houses of every committeeman in the country. Such a confession from on who was once entrusted with the powers of civil government, is a reproach to the character. But it is the wish and the declaration of a man whom anguish and disappointment have driven to despair, and who is daily decaying into the grave with constitutional rottenness.

There is not in the compass of language a sufficiency of words to express the baseness of your king, his ministry and his army. They have refined upon villainy till it wants a name. To the fiercer vices of former ages they have added the dregs and scummings of the most finished rascality, and are so completely sunk in serpentine deceit, that there is not left among them *one* generous enemy.

From such men and such masters may the gracious hand of Heaven preserve America! And though the sufferings she now endures are heavy and severe, they are like straws in the wind compared to the weight of evils she would feel under the government of your king, and his pensioned parliament.

There is something in meanness which excites a species of resentment that never subsides, and something in cruelty which stirs up the heart to the highest agony of human hatred; Britain hath filled up both these characters till no addition can be made, and hath not reputation left with us to obtain credit for the slightest promise. The will of God hath parted us, and the deed is registered for eternity. When she shall be a spot scarcely visible among the nations, America shall flourish, the favorite of Heaven and the friend of mankind.

For the domestic happiness of Britain and the peace of the world, I wish she had not a foot of land but what is circumscribed within her own island. Extent of dominion hath been her ruin, and instead of civilizing others hath brutalized herself. Her late reduction of India, under Clive and his successors, was not so properly a conquest as an extermination of mankind. She is the only power who could practice the prodigal barbarity of tying men to the mouths of loaded cannon and blowing them away. It happens that General Burgoyne, who made the report of that horrid transaction, in the house of commons, is now a prisoner with us, and though an enemy, I can appeal to him for the truth of it, being confident that he neither can nor will deny it. Yet Clive received the approbation of the last parliament.

When we take a survey of mankind, we cannot help cursing the wretch, who, to the unavoidable misfortunes of nature, shall wilfully add the calamities of war. One would think there were evils enough in the world without studying to increase them, and that life is sufficiently short without shaking the sand that measures it. The histories of Alexander, and Charles of Sweden, are the histories of human devils; a good man cannot think of their actions without abhorrence, nor of their deaths without rejoicing. To see the bounties of heaven destroyed, the beautiful face of nature laid waste, and the choicest works of creation and art tumbled into ruin, would fetch a curse from the soul of piety itself. But in this country the aggravation is heightened by a new combination of affecting circumstances. America was young, and, compared with other countries, was virtuous. None but a Herod of uncommon malice would have made war upon infancy and innocence: and none but a people of the most finished fortitude, dared, under those circumstances, to have resisted the tyranny. The natives, or their ancestors, had fled from the former oppressions of England, and with the industry of bees had changed a wilderness into a habitable world. To Britain they were indebted for nothing. The country was the gift of heaven, and God alone is their Lord and Sovereign.

The time, sir, will come when you, in a melancholy hour, shall reckon up your miseries by your murders in America. Life, with you, begins to wear a clouded aspect. The vision of pleasurable delusion is wearing away, and changing to the barren wild of age and sorrow. The poor reflection of having served your king will yield you no consolation in your parting moments. He will crumble to the same undistinguished ashes with yourself; and have sins enough of his own to answer for. It is not the farcical benedictions of a bishop, nor the cringing hypocrisy of a court of chaplains, nor the formality of an act of parliament, that can change guilt into innocence, or make the punishment *one* pang the less. You may, perhaps, be unwilling to be serious, but this destruction of the goods of Providence, this havoc of the human race, and this sowing the world with mischief, must be accounted for to him who made and governs it. To us they are only present sufferings, but to him they are deep rebellions.

If there is a sin superior to every other, it is that of willful and offensive war. Most other sins are circumscribed within narrow limits, that is, the power of *one* man cannot give them a very general extension, and many kinds of sins have only a mental existence from which no infection arises; but he who is the author of a war, lets loose the whole contagion of hell, and opens a vein that bleeds a nation to death. We leave it to England and Indians to boast of these honors; we feel no thirst for such savage glory; a nobler flame, a purer spirit animates America. She hath taken up the sword of virtuous defence; she hath bravely put herself between Tyranny and Freedom, between a curse and a blessing, determined to expel the one and protect the other.

It is the object only of war that makes it honorable. And if there was ever *a just* war since the world began, it is this in which America is now engaged. She invaded no land of yours. She hired no mercenaries to burn your towns, nor Indians to massacre their inhabitants. She wanted nothing from you, and was indebted for nothing to you: and thus circumstanced, her defence is honorable and her prosperity is certain.

Yet it is not on the *justice* only, but likewise on the *importance* of this cause that I ground my seemingly enthusiastic confidence of our success. The vast extension of America makes her of too much value in the scale of Providence, to be cast, like a pearl before swine, at the feet of an European island; and of much less consequence would it be that Britain were sunk in the sea than that America should miscarry. There hath been such a chain of extraordinary events in the discovery of this country at first, in the peopling and planting it afterwards, in the rearing and nursing it to its present state, and in the protection of it through the present war, that no man can doubt, but Providence hath some nobler end to accomplish, than the gratification of the petty elector of Hanover, or the ignorant and insignificant king of Britain.

As the blood of the martyrs hath been the seed of the Christian church, so the political persecutions of England will and hath already enriched America with industry, experience, union, and importance. Before the present era she was a mere chaos of uncemented colonies, individually exposed to the ravages of the Indians and the invasion of any power that Britain should be at war with. She had nothing that she could call her own. Her felicity depended upon accident. The convulsions of Europe might have thrown her from one conqueror to another, till she had been the slave of all, and ruined by every one; for until she had spirit enough to become her own master, there was no knowing to which master she should belong. *That* period, thank God, is past, and she is no longer the dependent, disunited colonies of Britain, but the Independent and United States of America,—knowing no master but heaven and herself. You, or your king, may call this "delusion," "rebellion," or what name you please. To us it is perfectly indifferent. The issue will determine the character, and time will give it a name as lasting as his own.

You have now, sir, tried the fate of three campaigns, and can fully declare to England, that nothing is to be got on your part, but blows and broken bones, and nothing on hers but waste of trade and credit, and an increase of poverty and taxes. You are now only where you might have been two years ago, without the loss of a single ship, and yet not a step more forward towards the conquest of the continent; because, as I have already hinted, "an army in a city can never be a conquering army." The full amount of your losses, since the beginning of the war, exceeds twenty thousand men, besides millions of treasure, for which you have nothing in exchange. Our expenses, though great, are circulated within ourselves. Yours is a direct sinking of money, and that from both ends at once; first, in hiring troops out of the nation, and in paying them afterwards, because the money in neither case can again return to Britain. We are already in possession of the prize, you only in pursuit of it. To us it is a real treasure, to you it would be only an empty triumph. Our expenses will repay themselves with tenfold interest, while yours entail upon you everlasting poverty.

Take a review, sir, of the ground which you have gone over, and let it teach you policy, if it cannot honesty. You stand but on a very tottering foundation. A change of the ministry in England may probably bring your measures into question, and your head to the block. Clive, with all his successes, had some difficulty in escaping, and yours, being all a war of losses, will afford you less pretensions, and your enemies more grounds for impeachment.

Go home, sir, and endeavor to save the remains of your ruined country, by a just representation of the madness of her measures. A few moments, well applied, may yet preserve her from political destruction. I am not one of those who wish to see Europe in a flame, because I am persuaded that such an event will not shorten the war. The rupture, at present, is confined between the two powers of America and England. England finds that she cannot conquer America, and America has no wish to conquer England. You are fighting for what you never can obtain, and we defending what we mean never to part with. A few words, therefore, settles the bargain. Let England mind her own business and we will mind ours. Govern yourselves, and we will govern ourselves. You may then trade where you please, unmolested by us, and we will trade where we please, unmolested by you; and such articles as we can purchase of each other, better than elsewhere, may be mutually done. If it were possible that you could carry on the war for twenty years you must still come to this point at last, or worse, and the sooner you think of it the better it will be for you. My official situation enables me to know the repeated insults which Britain is obliged to put up with from foreign powers, and the wretched shifts that she is driven to, to gloss them over. Her reduced strength and exhausted coffers in a three years' war with America, hath given a powerful superiority to France and Spain. She is not now a match for them. But if neither councils can prevail on her to think, nor sufferings awaken her to reason, she must e'en go on, till the honor of England becomes a proverb of contempt, and Europe dub her the Land of Fools.

I am, Sir, with every wish for an honorable peace,
Your friend, enemy, and countryman,

COMMON SENSE.

ᐁᕓᐅ

To the Inhabitants of America

WITH all the pleasure with which a man exchanges bad company for good, I take my leave of Sir William and return to you. It is now nearly three years since the tyranny of Britain received its first repulse by the arms of America. A period which has given birth to a new world, and erected a monument to the folly of the old.

I cannot help being sometimes surprised at the complimentary references which I have seen and heard made to ancient histories and transactions. The wisdom, civil governments, and sense of honor of the states of Greece and Rome, are frequently held up as objects of excellence and imitation. Mankind have lived to very little purpose, if, at this period of the world, they must go two or three thousand years back for lessons and examples. We do great injustice to ourselves by placing them in such a superior line. We have no just authority for it, neither can we tell why it is that we should suppose ourselves inferior.

Could the mist of antiquity be cleared away, and men and things be viewed as they really were, it is more than probable that they would admire us, rather than we them. America has surmounted a greater variety and combination of difficulties, than, I believe, ever fell to the share of any one people, in the same space of time, and has replenished the world with more useful knowledge and sounder maxims of civil government than were ever produced in any age before. Had it not been for America, there had been no such thing as freedom left throughout the whole universe. England hath lost hers in a long chain of right reasoning from wrong principles, and it is from this country, now, that she must learn the resolution to redress herself, and the wisdom how to accomplish it.

The Grecians and Romans were strongly possessed of the *spirit* of liberty but *not the principle*, for at the time that they were determined not to be slaves themselves, they employed their power to enslave the rest of mankind. But this distinguished era is blotted by no one misanthropical vice. In short, if the principle on which the cause is founded, the universal blessings that are to arise from it, the difficulties that accompanied it, the wisdom with which it has been debated, the fortitude by which it has been supported, the strength of the power which we had to oppose, and the condition in which we undertook it, be all taken in one view, we may justly style it the most virtuous and illustrious revolution that ever graced the history of mankind.

A good opinion of ourselves is exceedingly necessary in private life, but absolutely necessary in public life, and of the utmost importance in supporting national character. I have no notion of yielding the palm of the United States to any Grecians or Romans that were ever born. We have equalled the bravest in times of danger, and excelled the wisest in the construction of civil governments.

From this agreeable eminence let us take a review of present affairs. The spirit of corruption is so inseparably interwoven with British politics, that their ministry suppose all mankind are governed by the same motives. The have no idea of a people submitting even to temporary inconvenience from an attachment to rights and privileges. Their plans of business are calculated *by* the hour and *for* the hour, and are uniform in nothing but the corruption which gives them birth. They never had, neither have they at this time, any regular plan for the conquest of America by arms. They know not how to go about it, neither have they power to effect it if they did know. The thing is not within the compass of human practicability, for America is too extensive either to be fully conquered or *passively* defended. But she may be *actively* defended by defeating or making prisoners of the army that invades her. And this is the only system of defence that can be effectual in a large country.

There is something in a war carried on by invasion which makes it differ in circumstances from any other mode of war, because he who conducts it cannot tell whether the ground he gains be for him, or against him, when he first obtains it. In the winter of 1776, General Howe marched with an air of victory through the Jerseys, the consequence of which was his defeat;

and General Burgoyne at Saratoga experienced the same fate from the same cause. The Spaniards, about two years ago, were defeated by the Algerines in the same manner, that is, their first triumphs became a trap in which they were totally routed. And whoever will attend to the circumstances and events of a war carried on by invasion, will find, that any invader, in order to be finally conquered must first begin to conquer.

I confess myself one of those who believe the loss of Philadelphia to be attended with more advantages than injuries. The case stood thus: The enemy imagined Philadelphia to be of more importance to us than it really was; for we all know that it had long ceased to be a port: not a cargo of goods had been brought into it for near a twelvemonth, nor any fixed manufactories, nor even ship-building, carried on in it; yet as the enemy believed the conquest of it to be practicable, and to that belief added the absurd idea that the soul of all America was centered there, and would be conquered there, it naturally follows that their possession of it, by not answering the end proposed, must break up the plans they had so foolishly gone upon, and either oblige them to form a new one, for which their present strength is not sufficient, or to give over the attempt.

We never had so small an army to fight against, nor so fair an opportunity of final success as *now*. The death wound is already given. The day is ours if we follow it up. The enemy, by his situation, is within our reach, and by his reduced strength is within our power. The ministers of Britain may rage as they please, but our part is to conquer their armies. Let them wrangle andwelcome, but let it not draw our attention from the *one* thing needful. *Here, in this* spot is our business to be accomplished, our felicity secured. What we have now to do is as clear as light, and the way to do it is as straight as a line. It needs not to be commented upon, yet, in order to be perfectly understood, I will put a case that cannot admit of a mistake.

Had the armies under Generals Howe and Burgoyne been united, and taken post at Germantown, and had the northern army under General Gates been joined to that under General Washington, at Whitemarsh, the consequence would have been a general action; and if in that action we had killed and taken the same number of officers and men, that is, between nine and ten thousand, with the same quantity of artillery, arms, stores, &c., as have been taken at the northward, and obliged General Howe with the remains of his army, that is, with the same number he now commands, to take shelter in Philadelphia, we should certainly have thought ourselves the greatest heroes in the world; and should, as soon as the season permitted, have collected together all the force of the continent and laid siege to the city, for it requires a much greater force to besiege an enemy in a town than to defeat them in the field. The case *now* is just the same as if it had been produced by the means I have here supposed. Between nine and ten thousand have been killed and taken, all their stores are in our possession, and General Howe, in consequence of that victory, has thrown himself for shelter into Philadelphia.

He, or his trifling friend Galloway, may form what pretences they please, yet no just reason can be given for their going into winter quarters so early as the 19th of October, but their apprehensions of a defeat if they continued out, or their conscious inability of keeping the field with safety. I see no advantage which can arise to America by hunting the enemy from state to state. It is a triumph without a prize, and wholly unworthy the attention of a people determined to conquer. Neither can any state promise itself security while the enemy remains in a condition to transport themselves from one part of the continent to another. Howe, likewise, cannot conquer where we have no army to oppose, therefore any such removals in him are mean and cowardly, and reduces Britain to a common pilferer. If he retreats from Philadelphia, he will be despised; if he stays, he may be shut up and starved out, and the country, if he advances into it, may become his Saratoga. He has his choice of evils and we of opportunities. If he moves early, it is not only a sign but a proof that he expects no reinforcement, and his delays will prove that he either waits for the arrival of a plan to go upon, or force to execute it, or both; in *which* case our strength will increase more than his, therefore in *any* case we cannot be wrong if we do but proceed.

The particular condition of Pennsylvania deserves the attention of all the other states. Her military strength must not be estimated by the number of inhabitants. Here are men of all nations, characters, professions and interests. Here are the firmest whigs, surviving, like sparks in the ocean, unquenched and uncooled in the midst of discouragement and disaffection. Here are men losing their all with cheerfulness, and collecting fire and fortitude from the flames of their own estates. Here are others skulking in secret, many making a market of the times, and numbers who are changing to whig and tory with the circumstances of every day.

It is by mere dint of fortitude and perseverance that the whigs of this state have been able to maintain so good a countenance, and do even what they have done. We want help, and the sooner it can arrive the more effectual it will be. The invaded state, be it which it may, will always feel an additional burden upon its bank, and be hard set to support its civil power with sufficient authority; and this difficulty will always rise or fall, in proportion as the other states throw in their assistance to the common cause.

The enemy will most probably make many manœuvres at the opening of this campaign, to amuse and draw off the attention of the several states from the *one thing needful*. We may expect to hear of alarms and pretended expeditions to *this* place and *that* place, to the Southward, the Eastward and the Northward, all intended to prevent our forming into one formidable body. The less the enemy's strength is, the more subtleties of this kind will they make use of. Their existence depends upon it, because the force of America, when collected, is sufficient to swallow their present army up. It is therefore our business to make short work of it, by bending our whole attention to *this one principal point*, for the instant that the main body under General Howe is defeated, all the inferior alarms throughout the continent, like so many shadows, will follow his downfall.

The only way to finish a war with the least possible bloodshed, or perhaps without any, is to collect an army, against the power of which the enemy shall have no chance. By not doing this, we prolong the war, and double both the calamities and the expenses of it. What a rich and happy country would America be, were she, by a vigorous exertion, to reduce Howe as she has reduced Burgoyne. Her currency would rise to millions beyond its present value. Every man would be rich, and every man would have it in his power to be happy. And why not do these things? What is there to hinder? America is her own mistress and can do what she pleases.

If we had not at this time a man in the field, we could, nevertheless, raise an army in a few weeks sufficient to overwhelm all the force which General Howe at present commands. Vigor and determination will do any thing and every thing. We began the war with this kind of spirit, why not end it with the same? Here, gentlemen, is the enemy. Here is the army. The interest, the happiness of all America, is centered in this half ruined spot. Come on and help us. Here are laurels, come and share them. Here are tories, come and help us to expel them. Here are whigs that will make you welcome, and enemies that dread your coming.

The worst of all policy is that of doing things by halves. Penny wise and pound foolish, has been the ruin of thousands. The present spring, if rightly improved, will free us from all our troubles, and save us the expense of millions. We have now only one army to cope with. No opportunity can be fairer; no prospect more promising. I shall conclude this paper with a few outlines of a plan, either for filling up the battalions with expedition, or for raising an additional force, for any limited time, on any sudden emergency.

That in which every man is interested, is every man's duty to support. And any burden which falls equally on all men, and from which every man is to receive an equal benefit, is consistent with the most perfect ideas of liberty. I would wish to revive something of that virtuous ambition which first called America into the field. Then every man was eager to do his part, and perhaps the principal reason why we have in any degree fallen therefrom, is because we did not set a sufficient value by it at. first, but left it to blaze out of itself, instead of regulating and preserving it by just proportions of rest and service.

Suppose any state whose number of effective inhabitants was 80,000, should be required to furnish 3,200 men towards the defence of the continent, on any sudden emergency.

First, Let the whole number of effective inhabitants be divided into hundreds; then if each of those hundreds turn out four men, the whole number of 3,200 will be had.

Secondly, Let the names of each hundred men be entered in a book, and let four dollars be collected from each man, with as much more as any of the gentlemen, whose abilities can afford it, shall please to throw in, which gifts likewise shall be entered against the donors' names.

Thirdly, Let the sums so collected be offered as a present, over and above the bounty of twenty dollars, to any four who may be inclined to propose themselves as volunteers. If more than four offer, the majority of the subscribers present shall determine which; if none offer, then four out of the hundred shall be taken by lot, who shall be entitled to the said sums, and shall either go, or provide others that will, in the space of six days.

Fourthly, As it will always happen, that in the space of ground on which an hundred men shall live, there will be always a number of persons who, by age and infirmity, are incapable of doing personal service, and as such persons are generally possessed of the greatest part of the property in any country, their portion of service, therefore, will be to furnish each man with a blanket, which will make a regimental coat, jacket, and breeches, or clothes in lieu thereof, and another for a watch cloak, and two pair of shoes—for however choice people may be of these things matters not in cases of this kind-—those who live always in houses can find many ways to keep themselves warm, but it is a shame and a sin to suffer a soldier in the field to want a blanket while there is one in the country.

Should the clothing not be wanted, the superannuated or infirm persons possessing property, may, in lieu thereof, throw in their money subscriptions towards increasing the bounty; for though age will naturally exempt a person from personal service, it cannot exempt him from his share of the charge, because the men are raised for the defence of property and liberty, jointly.

There never was a scheme against which objections might not be raised. But this alone is not a sufficient reason for rejection. The only line to judge truly upon, is to draw out and admit all the objections which can fairly be made, and place against them all the contrary qualities, conveniencies and advantages, then by striking a balance you come at the true character of any scheme, principle or position.

The most material advantages of the plan here proposed are, ease, expedition, and cheapness; yet the men so raised get a much larger bounty than is any where at present given; because all the expenses, extravagance, and consequent idleness of recruiting are saved or prevented. The country incurs no new debt, nor interest thereon; the whole matter being all settled at once and entirely done with. It is a subscription answering all the purposes of a tax, without either the charge or trouble of collecting. The men are ready for the field with the greatest possible expedition, because it becomes the duty of the inhabitants themselves, in every part of the country, to find their proportion of men, instead of leaving it to a recruiting sergeant, who, be he ever so industrious, cannot know always where to apply.

I do not propose this as a regular digested plan, neither will the limits of this paper admit of any further remarks upon it. I believe it to be a hint capable of much improvement, and as such submit it to the public.

COMMON SENSE.
Lancaster, March 21, 1778.

THE CRISIS
NUMBER VI

To the Earl of Carlisle, General Clinton, and William Eden, Esq., British Commissioners, at New York

There which is a dignity in the warm passions of a whig, which is never to be found in the cold malice of a tory. In the one, nature is only heated—in the other she is poisoned. The instant the former has it in his power to punish, he feels a disposition to forgive; but the canine venom of the latter knows no relief but revenge. This general distinction will, I believe, apply in all cases, and suit as well the meridian of England as America.

As I presume your last proclamation will undergo the strictures of other pens, I shall confine my remarks to only a few parts thereof. All that you have said might have been comprised in half the compass. It is tedious and unmeaning, and only a repetition of your former follies, with here and there an offensive aggravation. Your cargo of pardons will have no market—It is unfashionable to look at them—even speculation is at an end. They have become a perfect drug, and no way calculated for the climate.

In the course of your proclamation you say, "The policy as well as the *benevolence of Great Britain* have thus far checked the extremes of war, when they tended to distress a people still considered as their fellow subjects, and to desolate a country shortly to become again a source of mutual advantage." What you mean by "the *benevolence* of Great Britain" is to me inconceivable. To put a plain question; do you consider your-selves men or devils? For until this point is settled, no deter-minate sense can be put upon the expression. You have already equalled, and in many cases excelled, the savages of either Indies; and if you have yet a cruelty in store, you must have imported it, unmixed with every human material, from the original warehouse of hell.

To the interposition of Providence, and her blessings on our endeavors, and not to *British benevolence*, are we indebted for the short chain that limits your ravages. Remember. you do not at this time, command a foot of land on the continent of America. Staten Island, York Island, a small part of Long Island, and Rhode Island, circumscribe your power; and even those you hold at the expense of the West Indies. To avoid a defeat, and prevent a desertion of your troops, you have taken up your quarters in holes and corners of inaccessible security; and in order to conceal what every one can perceive, you now endeavor to impose your weakness upon us for an act of mercy. If you think to succeed by such shadowy devices, you are but infants in the political world; you have the A, B, C, of stratagem yet to learn, and are wholly ignorant of the people you have to contend with. Like men in a state of intoxication, you forget that the rest of the world have eyes, and that the same stupidity which conceals you from yourselves exposes you to their satire and contempt.

The paragraph which I have quoted, stands as an introduc-tion to the following: "But when that country (America) pro-fesses the unnatural design, not only of estranging herself from us, but of mortgaging herself and her resources to our enemies, the whole contest is changed: and the question is how far Great Britain may, by every means in her power, destroy or render useless a connection contrived for her ruin, and the aggrandizement of France. Under such circumstances, the laws of self-preservation must direct the conduct of Britain, and if the British colonies are to become an accession to France, will direct her to render that accession of as little avail as possible to her enemy."

I consider you in this declaration, like madmen biting in the hour of death. It contains likewise a fraudulent meanness; for, in order to justify a barbarous conclusion, you have advanced a false position. The treaty we have formed with France is open, noble, and generous. It is true policy, founded on sound philosophy, and neither a surrender or mortgage, as you would scandalously insinuate. I have seen every article, and speak from positive knowledge. In France, we have found an affectionate friend and faithful ally; in Britain, we have found nothing but tyranny, cruelty, and infidelity.

But the happiness is, that the mischief you threaten is not in your power to execute; and if it were, the punishment would return upon you in a ten-fold degree. The humanity of America hath hitherto restrained her from acts of retaliation, and the affection she retains for many individuals in England, who have fed, clothed and comforted her prisoners, has, to the present day, warded off her resentment, and operated as a screen to the whole. But even these considerations must cease, when national objects interfere and oppose them. Repeated aggravations will provoke a retort, and policy justify the measure. We mean now to take you seriously up upon your own ground and principle, and as you do, so shall you be done by.

You ought to know, gentlemen, that England and Scotland, are far more exposed to incendiary desolation than America, in her present state, can possibly be. We occupy a country, with but few towns, and whose riches consist in land and annual produce. The two last can suffer but little, and that only within a very limited compass. In Britain it is otherwise. Her wealth lieschiefly in cities and large towns, the depositories of manufactures and fleets of merchantmen.—There is not a nobleman's country seat but may be laid in ashes by a single person. Your own may probably contribute to the proof: in short, there is no evil which cannot be returned when you come to incendiary mischief.—The ships in the Thames, may certainly be as easily set on fire, as the temporary bridge was a few years ago; yet of that affair no discovery was ever made; and the loss you would sustain by such an event, executed at a proper season, is infinitely greater than any you can inflict. The East India house, and the bank, neither are, nor can be secure from this sort of destruction, and, as Dr. Price justly observes, a fire at the latter would bankrupt the nation. It has never been the custom of France and England when at war, to make those havocs on each other, because the ease with which they could retaliate rendered it as impolitic as if each had destroyed his own.

But think not, gentlemen, that our distance secures you, or our invention fails us. We can much easier accomplish such a point than any nation in Europe. We talk the same language, dress in the same habit, and appear with the same manners as yourselves. We can pass from one part of England to another unsuspected; many of us are as well acquainted with the country as you are, and should you impoliticly provoke us, you will most assuredly lament the effects of it. Mischiefs of this kind require no army to execute them. The means are obvious, and the opportunities unguardable. I hold up a warning to your senses, if you have any left, and "to the unhappy people likewise, whose affairs are committed to you."* Call not with the

---

* General Clinton's letter to Congress.

rancor of an enemy, but the earnestness of a friend, on the deluded people of England, lest, between your blunders and theirs, they sink beneath the evils contrived for us.

"He who lives in a glass house," says a Spanish proverb, "should never begin throwing stones." This, gentlemen, is exactly your case, and you must be the most ignorant of mankind, or suppose us so, not to see on which side the balance of accounts will fall. There are many other modes of retaliation, which, for several reasons, I choose not to mention. But be assured of this, that the instant you put your threat in execution, a counter-blow will follow it. If you openly profess yourselves savages, it is high time we should treat you as such, and if nothing but distress can recover you to reason, to punish will become an office of charity.

While your fleet lay last winter in the Delaware, I offered my service to the Pennsylvania navy-board then at Trenton, as one who would make a party with them, or any four or five gentlemen, on an expedition down the river to set fire to it, and though it was not then accepted, nor the thing personally attempted, it is more than probable that your own folly will provoke a much more ruinous act. Say not when the mischief is done, that you had not warning, and remember that we do not begin it, but mean to repay it. Thus much for your savage and impolitic threat.

In another part of your proclamation you say, "But if the honors of a military life are become the object of the Americans, let them seek those honors under the banners of their rightful sovereign, and in fighting the battles of the united British empire, against our late mutual and natural enemies." Surely! the union of absurdity with madness was never marked in more distinguishable lines than these. Your rightful sovereign, as you call him, may do well enough for you, who dare not inquire into the humble capacities of the man; but we, who estimate persons and things by their real worth, cannot suffer our judgments to be so imposed upon; and, unless it is your wish to see him exposed, it ought to be your endeavor to keep him out of sight. The less you have to say about him the better. We have done with him, and that ought to be answer enough. You have been often told so. Strange! that the answer must he so often repeated. You go a begging with your king as with a brat, or with some unsalable commodity you were tired of; and though everybody tells you "no, no," still you keep hawking him about. But there is one that will have him in a little time, and as we have no inclination to disappoint you of a customer, we bid nothing for him.

The impertinent folly of the paragraph that I have just quoted, deserves no other notice than to be laughed at and thrown by, but the principle on which it is founded is detestable. We are invited to submit to a man who has attempted by every cruelty to destroy us, and to join him in making war against France, who is already at war against him for our support.

Can Bedlam, in concert with Lucifer, form a more mad and devilish request? Were it possible a people could sink into such apostacy they would deserve to be swept from the earth like the inhabitants of Sodom and Gomorrah. The proposition is an universal affront to the rank which man holds in the creation, and an indignity to him who placed him there. It supposes him made up without a spark of honor, and under no obligation to God or man.

What sort of men or Christians must you suppose the Americans to be, who, after seeing their most humble petitions insultingly rejected—the most grievous laws passed to distress them in every quarter—an undeclared war let loose upon them, and Indians and Negroes invited to the slaughter—who, after seeing their kinsmen murdered, their fellow citizens starved to death in prisons, and their houses and property destroyed and burned,—who, after the most serious appeals to heaven—the most solemn abjuration by oath of all government connected with you, and the most heart-felt pledges and protestation of faith to each other—and who, after soliciting the friendship, and entering into alliances with other nations, should at last break through all these obligations, civil and divine, by complying with your horrid and infernal proposal? Ought we ever after to be considered as a part of the human race? or, ought we not rather to be blotted from the society of mankind, and become a spectacle of misery to the world? But there is something in corruption, which, like a jaundiced eye, transfers the color of itself to the object it looks upon, and sees every thing stained and impure; for unless you were capable of such conduct yourselves, you could never have supposed such a character in us. The offer fixes your infamy. It exhibits you as a nation without faith; with whom oaths and treaties are considered as trifles, and the breaking them as the breaking of a bubble. Regard to decency, or to rank, might have taught you better; or pride inspired you, though virtue could not. There is not left a step in the degradation of character to which you can now descend; you have put your foot on the ground floor, and the key of the dungeon is turned upon you.

That the invitation may want nothing of being a complete monster, you have thought proper to finish it with an assertion which has no foundation, either in fact or philosophy; and as Mr. Ferguson, your secretary, is a man of letters, and has made civil society his study, and published a treatise on that subject, I address this part to him.

In the close of the paragraph last quoted, France is styled

the "natural enemy" of England, and by way of lugging us into some strange idea, she is styled "the late mutual and natural enemy" of both countries. I deny that she ever was the natural enemy of either; and that there does not exist in nature such a principle. The expression is an unmeaning barbarism, and wholly unphilosophical, when applied to beings of the same species, let their station in the creation be what it may. We have a perfect idea of a natural enemy when we think of the devil, because the enmity is perpetual, unalterable, and unabatable. It admits neither of peace, truce, or treaty; consequently the warfare is eternal, and therefore it is natural. But man with man cannot arrange in the same opposition. Their quarrels are accidental and equivocally created. They become friends or enemies as the change of temper, or the cast of interest inclines them. The Creator of man did not constitute them the natural enemy of each other. He has not made any one order of beings so. Even wolves may quarrel, still they herd together. If any two nations are so, then must all nations be so, otherwise it is not nature but custom, and the offence frequently originates with the accuser. England is as truly the natural enemy of France, as France is of England, and perhaps more so. Separated from the rest of Europe, she has contracted an unsocial habit of manners, and imagines in others the jealousy she creates in herself. Never long satisfied with peace, she supposes the discontent universal, and buoyed up with her own importance, conceives herself the only object pointed at. The expression has been often used, and always with a fraudulent design; for when the idea of a natural enemy is conceived, it prevents all other enquiries, and the real cause of the quarrel is hidden in the universality of the conceit. Men start at the notion of a natural enemy, and ask no other question. The cry obtains credit like the alarm of a mad dog, and is one of those kind of tricks, which, by operating on the common passions, secures their interest through their folly.

But we, sir, are not to be thus imposed upon. We live in a large world, and have extended our ideas beyond the limits and prejudices of an island. We hold out the right hand of friendship to all the universe, and we conceive that there is a sociality in the manners of France, which is much better disposed to peace and negotiation than that of England, and until the latter becomes more civilized, she cannot expect to live long at peace with any power. Her common language is vulgar and offensive, and children with their milk suck in the rudiments of insult—"The arm of Britain! The mighty arm of Britain! Britain that shakes the earth to its centre and its poles! The scourge of France! The terror of the world! That governs with a nod, and pours down vengeance like a God." This language neither makes a nation great or little; but it shows a savageness of manners, and has a tendency to keep national animosity alive. The entertainments of the stage are calculated to the same end, and almost every public exhibition is tinctured with insult. Yet England is always in dread of France. Terrified at the apprehension of an invasion. Suspicious of being outwitted in a treaty, and privately cringing, though she is publicly offending. Let her therefore, reform her manners and do justice, and she will find the idea of a natural enemy to be only a phantom of her own imagination.

Little did I think, at this period of the war, to see a proclamation which could promise you no one useful purpose whatever, and tend only to expose you. One would think you were just awakened from a four years' dream, and knew nothing of what had passed in the interval. Is this a time to be offering pardons, or renewing the long forgotten subjects of charters and taxation? Is it worth your while, after every force has

failed you, to retreat under the shelter of argument and persuasion? Or can you think that we, with nearly half your army
prisoners, and in alliance with France, are to be begged or
threatened into submission by a piece of paper? But as commissioners, each at a hundred pounds sterling a week, you conceive yourselves bound to do something, and the genius of ill
fortune told you, you must write. For my own part, I have not
put pen to paper these several months. Convinced of our superiority by the issue of every campaign, I was inclined to hope,
that that which all the rest of the world now see, would become
visible to you, and therefore felt unwilling to ruffle your
temper by fretting you with repetitions and discoveries. There
have been intervals of hesitation in your conduct, from which
it seemed a pity to disturb you, and a charity to leave you to
yourselves. You have often stopped, as if you intended to
think, but your thoughts have ever been too early or too late.

There was a time when Britain disdained to answer, or
even hear a petition from America. That time is past, and she
in her turn is petitioning our acceptance. We now stand on
higher ground, and offer her peace; and the time will come
when she, perhaps in vain, will ask it from us. The latter case
is as probable as the former ever was. She cannot refuse to
acknowledge our independence with greater obstinacy than
she before refused to repeal her laws; and if America alone
could bring her to the one, united with France she will reduce
her to the other. There is something in obstinacy which differs
from every other passion. Whenever it fails it never recovers,
but either breaks like iron, or crumbles sulkily away like a
fractured arch. Most other passions have their periods of
fatigue and rest—their suffering and their cure; but obstinacy
has no resource, and the first wound is mortal. You have
already begun to give it up, and you will, from the natural con-

struction of the vice, find yourselves both obliged and inclined to do so.

If you look back you see nothing but loss and disgrace. If you look forward the same scene continues, and the close is an impenetrable gloom. You may plan and execute little mischiefs, but are they worth the expense they cost you, or will such partial evils have any effect on the general cause? Your expedition to Egg Harbor, will be felt at a distance like an attack upon a hen-roost, and expose you in Europe, with a sort of childish frenzy. Is it worth while to keep an army to protect you in writing proclamations, or to get once a year into winter-quarters? Possessing yourselves of towns is not conquest, but convenience, and in which you will one day or other be trepanned. Your retreat from Philadelphia, was only a timely escape, and your next expedition may be less fortunate.

It would puzzle all the politicians in the universe to conceive what you stay for, or why you should have staid so long. You are prosecuting a war in which you confess you have neither object nor hope, and that conquest, could it be effected, would not repay the charges. In the meanwhile, the rest of your affairs are running into ruin, and a European war kindling against you. In such a situation, there is neither doubt or difficulty; the first rudiments of reason will determine the choice, for if peace can be procured with more advantages than even a conquest can be obtained, he must be an idiot indeed that hesitates.

But you are probably buoyed up by a set of wretched mortals, who, having deceived themselves, are cringing with the duplicity of a spaniel for a little temporary bread. Those men will tell you just what you please. It is their interest to amuse, in order to lengthen out their protection. They study to keep you amongst them for that very purpose; and in proportion as you disrgard their advice, and grow callous to their complaints, they will stretch into improbability, and season their flattery the higher. Characters like these, are to be found in every country, and every country will despise them.

COMMON SENSE.
Philadelphia, Oct. 20, 1773.

THE CRISIS
NUMBER VII

To the People of England

THERE are stages in the business of serious life in which to amuse is cruel, but to deceive is to destroy; and it is of little consequence, in the conclusion, whether men deceive themselves, or submit, by a kind of mutual consent, to the impositions of each other. That England has long been under the influence of delusion or mistake, needs no other proof than the unexpected and wretched situation she is now involved in; and so powerful has been the influence, that no provision was ever made or thought of against the misfortune, because the possibility of its happening was never conceived.

The general and successful resistance of America, the conquest of Burgoyne, and a war in France, were treated in parliament as the dreams of a discontented opposition, or a distempered imagination. They were beheld as objects unworthy of a serious thought, and the bare intimation of them afforded the ministry a triumph of laughter. Short triumph indeed! For every thing which has been predicted has happened, and all that was promised has failed. A long series of politics so remarkably distinguished by a succession of misfortunes, without one alleviating turn, must certainly have something in it systematically wrong. It is sufficient to awaken the most credulous into suspicion, and the most obstinate into thought. Either the means in your power are insufficient, or the measures ill planned; either the execution has been bad, or the thing attempted impracticable; or, to speak more emphatically, either you are not able, or heaven is not willing. For, why is it that you have not conquered us? Who, or what has prevented you? You have had every opportunity that you could desire, and succeeded to your utmost wish in every preparatory means. Your fleets and armies have arrived in America without an accident. No uncommon misfortune hath intervened. No foreign nation hath interfered until the time which you had allotted for victory was past. The opposition, either in or out of parliament, neither disconcerted your measures, retarded or diminished your force. They only foretold your fate. Every ministerial scheme was carried with as high a hand as if the whole nation had been unanimous. Every thing wanted was asked for, and every thing asked for was granted.

A greater force was not within the compass of your abilities to send, and the time you sent it was of all others the most favorable. You were then at rest with the whole world beside. You had the range of every court in Europe uncontradicted by us. You amused us with a tale of commissioners of peace, and under that disguise collected a numerous army and came almost unexpectedly upon us. The force was much greater than we looked for; and that which we had to oppose it with was unequal in numbers, badly armed, and poorly disciplined; beside which, it was embodied only for a short time, and expired within a few months after your arrival. We had governments to form; measures to concert; an army to raise and train, and every necessary article to import or to create. Our non-importation scheme had exhausted our stores, and your command by sea intercepted our supplies. We were a people unknown, and unconnected with the political world, and strangers to the disposition of foreign powers. Could you possibly wish for a more favorable conjunction of circumstances? Yet all these have happened and passed away, and, as it were, left you with a laugh. They are likewise events of such an original nativity as can never happen again, unless a new world should arise from the ocean.

If any thing can be a lesson to presumption, surely the circumstances of this war will have their effect. Had Britain been defeated by any European power, her pride would have drawn consolation from the importance of her conquerors; but in the present case, she is excelled by those she affected to despise, and her own opinions retorting upon herself, become an aggravation of her disgrace. Misfortune and experience are lost upon mankind, when they produce neither reflection nor reformation. Evils, like poisons, have their uses, and there are diseases which no other remedy can reach. It has been the crime and folly of England to suppose herself invincible, and that, without acknowledging or perceiving that a full third of her strength was drawn from the country she is now at war with. The arm of Britain has been spoken of as the arm of the Almighty, and she has lived of late as if she thought the whole world was created for her diversion. Her politics, instead of civilizing, has tended to brutalize mankind, and under the vain, unmeaning title of "Defender of the Faith," she has made war like an Indian against the religion of humanity. Her cruelties in the East Indies will *never* be forgotten; and it is somewhat remarkable that the produce of that ruined country, transported to America, should there kindle up a war to punish the destroyer. The chain in continued, though with a kind of mysterious uniformity both in the crime and the punishment. The latter runs parallel with the former, and time and fate will give it a perfect illustration.

Where information is withheld, ignorance becomes a reasonable excuse; and one would charitably hope that the people of England do not encourage cruelty from choice but from mistake. Their recluse situation, surrounded by the sea, preserves them from the calamities of war, and keeps them in the dark as to the conduct of their own armies. They see not, therefore they feel not. They tell the tale that is told them and believe it, and accustomed to no other news than their own, they receive it, stripped of its horrors and prepared for the palate of the nation, through the channel of the *London Gazette*. They are made to believe that their generals and armies differ from those of other nations, and have nothing of rudeness or barbarity in them. They suppose them what they wish them to be. They feel a disgrace in thinking otherwise, and naturally encourage the belief from a partiality to themselves. There was a time when I felt the same prejudices, and reasoned from the same errors; but experience, sad and painful experience, has thought me better. What the conduct of former armies was, I know not, but what the conduct of the present is, I well know. It is low, cruel, indolent and profligate; and had the people of America no other cause for separation than what the army has occasioned, that alone is cause sufficient.

The field of politics in England is far more extensive than that of news. Men have a right to reason for themselves, and though they cannot contradict the intelligence in the *London Gazette*, they may frame upon it what sentiments they please. But the misfortune is, that a general ignorance has prevailed over the whole nation respecting America. The ministry and minority have both been wrong. The former was always so; the latter only lately so. Politics, to be executively right, must have a unity of means and time, and a defect in either overthrows the whole. The ministry rejected the plans of the minority while they were practicable, and joined in them when they became impracticable. From wrong measures they got into wrong time, and have now completed the circle of absurdity by closing it upon themselves.

It was my fate to come to America a few months before the breaking out of hostilities. I found the disposition of the people such, that they might have been led by a thread and governed by a reed. Their suspicion was quick and penetrating, but their attachment to Britain was obstinate, and it was at that time a kind of treason to speak against it. They disliked the ministry, but they esteemed the nation. Their idea of grievance operated without resentment, and their single object was reconciliation. Bad as I believed the ministry to be, I never conceived them capable of a measure so rash and wicked as the commencing of hostilities; much less did I imagine the nation would encourage it. I viewed the dispute as a kind of law-suit, in which I supposed the parties would find a way either to decide or settle it. I had no thoughts of independence or of arms. The world could not then have persuaded me that I should be either a soldier or an author. If I had any talents for either, they were buried in me, and might ever have continued so, had not the necessity of the times dragged and driven them into action. I had formed my plan of life, and conceiving myself happy, wished every body else so. But when the country, into which I had just put my foot, was set on fire about my ears, it was time to stir. It was time for every man to stir. Those who had been long settled had something to defend; those who had just come had something to pursue; and the call and the concern was equal and universal. For in a country where all men were once adventurers, the difference of a few years in their arrival could make none in their right.

The breaking out of hostilities opened a new suspicion in the politics of America, which though at that time very rare, has been since proved to be very right. What I allude to is, "a secret and fixed determination in the British cabinet to annex America to the crown of England as a conquered country." If this be taken as the object, then the whole line of conduct pursued by the ministry, though rash in its origin and ruinous in its consequences, is nevertheless uniform and consistent in its parts. It applies to every case and resolves every difficulty. But if taxation or any thing else be taken in its room, then is there no proportion between the object and the charge. Nothing but the whole soil and property of the country can be placed, as a possible equivalent against the millions which the ministry expended. No taxes raised in America could possibly repay it. A revenue of two millions sterling a year would not discharge the sum and interest accumulated thereon in twenty years.

Reconciliation never appears to have been the wish or the object of the administration. They looked on conquest as certain and infallible, and under that persuasion sought to drive the Americans into what they might style a general rebellion, and then, crushing them with arms in their hands, reap the rich harvest of a general confiscation, and silence them for ever. The dependants at court were too numerous to be provided for in England. The market for plunder in the East Indies was over; and the profligacy of government required that a new mine should be opened, and that mine could be no other than America conquered and forfeited. They had no where else to go. Every other channel was drained; and extravagance, with the thrift of a drunkard, was gaping for supplies.

If the ministry deny this to have been their plan, it becomes them to explain what was their plan. For either they have abused us in coveting property they never labored for, or they have abused you in expending an amazing sum upon an incompetent object. Taxation, as I mentioned before, could never be worth the charge of obtaining it by arms; and any kind of formal obedience which America could have made, would have weighed with the lightness of a laugh against such a load of expense. It is therefore most probable, that the ministry will at last justify their policy by their dishonesty, and openly declare, that their original design was conquest: and in this case, it well becomes the people of England to consider how far the nation would have been benefited by the success.

In a general view, there are few conquests that repay the charge of making them, and mankind are pretty well convinced that it can never be worth their while to go to war for profit's sake. If they are made war upon, their country invaded, or their existence at stake, it is their duty to defend and preserve themselves, but in every other light, and from every other cause, is war inglorious and detestable. But to return to the case in question—

When conquests are made of foreign countries, it is supposed that the *commerce* and *dominion* of the country which made them are extended. But this could neither be the object nor the consequence of the present war. You enjoyed the whole commerce before. It could receive no possible addition by a conquest, but on the contrary, must diminish as the inhabitants were reduced in numbers and wealth. You had the same *dominion* over the country which you used to have, and had no complaint to make against her for breach of any part of the contract between you or her, or contending against any established custom, commercial, political or territorial. The country and commerce were both your own when you *began* to conquer, in the same manner and form as they had been your own an hundred years before. Nations have sometimes been induced to make conquests for the sake of reducing the power of their enemies, or bringing it to a balance with their own. But this could be no part of your plan. No foreign authority was claimed here, neither was any such authority suspected by you, or acknowledged or imagined by us. What then, in the name of heaven, could you go to war for? or what chance could you possibly have in the event, but either to hold the same country which you held before, and that in a much worse condition, or to lose, with an amazing expense, what you might have retained without a farthing of charges.

War never can be the interest of a trading nation, any more than quarreling can be profitable to a man in business. But to make war with those who trade with us, is like setting a bull dog upon a customer at the shop doors. The least degree of common sense shows the madness of the latter, and it will apply with the same force of conviction to the former. Piratical nations, having neither commerce or commodities of their own to lose, may make war upon all the world, and lucratively find their account in it; but it is quite otherwise with Britain: for, besides the stoppage of trade in time of war, she exposes more of her own property to be lost, than she has the chance of taking from others. Some ministerial gentlemen in parliament have mentioned the greatness of her trade as an apology for the greatness of her loss. This is miserable politics indeed! because it ought to have been given as a reason for her not engaging in a war at first. The coast of America commands the West India trade almost as effectually as the coast of Africa does that of the Straits; and England can no more carry on the former without the consent of America, than she can the latter without a Mediterranean pass.

In whatever light the war with America is considered upon commercial principles, it is evidently the interest of the people of England not to support it; and why it has been supported so long, against the clearest demonstrations of truth and national advantage, is to me, and must be to all the reasonable world, a matter of astonishment. Perhaps it may be said that I live in America, and write this from interest. To this I reply, that my principles are universal. My attachment is to all the world, and not, to any particular part, and if what I advance is right, then no matter where or who it comes from.

We have given the proclamation of your commissioners a currency in our newspapers, and I have no doubt you will give this a place in yours. To oblige and be obliged is fair.

Before I dismiss this part of my address, I shall mention one more circumstance in which I think the people of England have been equally mistaken: and then proceed to other matters.

There is such an idea existing in the world, as that of *national honor*, and this falsely understood, is oftentimes the cause of war. In a Christian and philosophical sense, mankind seem to have stood still at individual civilization, and to retain as nations all the original rudeness of nature. Peace by treaty is only a cessation of violence for a reformation of sentiment. It is a substitute for a principle that is wanting and ever will be wanting till the idea of *national honor* be rightly understood. As individuals we profess ourselves Christians, but as nations we are heathens, Romans, and what not. I remember the late Admiral Saunders declaring in the house of commons, and that in a time of peace, "That the city of Madrid laid in ashes was not a sufficient atonement for the Spaniards taking off the ruder of an English sloop of war." I do not ask whether this is Christianity or morality, I ask whether it is decency? whether it is proper language for a nation to use? In private life we call it by the plain name of bullying, and the elevation of rank cannot alter its character. It is, I think, exceedingly easy to define what ought to be understood by national honor; for that which is the best character for an individual is the best character for a nation; and wherever the latter exceeds or falls beneath the former, there is a departure from the line of true greatness.

I have thrown out this observation with a design of applying it to Great Britain. Her ideas of national honor, seem devoid of that benevolence of heart, that universal expansion of philanthropy, and that triumph over the rage of vulgar prejudice, without which man is inferior to himself, and a companion of common animals. To know whom she shall regard or dislike, she asks what country they are of, what religion they profess, and what property they enjoy. Her idea of national honor seems to consist in national insult, and that to be a great people, is to be neither a Christian, a philosopher, or a gentleman, but to threaten with the rudeness of a bear, and to devour with the ferocity of a lion. This perhaps may sound harsh and uncourtly, but it is too true, and the more is the pity.

I mention this only as her general character. But towards America she has observed no character at all; and destroyed by her conduct what she assumed in her title. She set out with the title of parent, or mother country. The association of ideas which naturally accompany this expression, are filled with every thing that is fond, tender and forbearing. They have an energy peculiar to themselves, and, overlooking the accidental attachment of common affections, apply with infinite softness to the first feelings of the heart. It is a political term which every mother can feel the force of, and every child can judge of. It needs no painting of mine to set it off, for nature only can do it justice.

But has any part of your conduct to America corresponded with the title you set up? If in your general national character you are unpolished and severe, in this you are inconsistent and unnatural, and you must have exceedingly false notions of national honor, to suppose that the world can admire a want of humanity, or that national honor depends on the violence of resentment, the inflexibility of temper, or the vengeance of execution.

I would willingly convince you, and that with as much

temper as the times will suffer me to do, that as you opposed your own interest by quarreling with us, so likewise your national honor, rightly conceived and understood, was no ways called upon to enter into a war with America. Had you studied true greatness of heart, the first and fairest ornament of mankind, you would have acted directly contrary to all that you have done, and the world would have ascribed it to a generous cause; besides which, you had (though with the assistance of this country) secured a powerful name by the last war. You were known and dreaded abroad; and it would have been wise in you to have suffered the world to have slept undisturbed under that idea. It was to you a force existing without expense. It produced to you all the advantages of real power; and you were stronger through the universality of that charm, than any future fleets and armies may probably make you. Your greatness was so secured and interwoven with your silence, that you ought never to have awakened mankind, and had nothing to do but to be quiet. Had you been true politicians you would have seen all this, and continued to draw from the magic of a name, the force and authority of a nation.

Unwise as you were in breaking the charm, you were still more unwise in the manner of doing it. Sampson only told the secret, but you have performed the operation; you have shaven your own head, and wantonly thrown away the locks. America was the hair from which the charm was drawn that infatuated the world. You ought to have quarreled with no power; but with her upon no account. You had nothing to fear from any condescension you might make. You might have humored her, even if there had been no justice in her claims, without any risk to your reputation; for Europe, fascinated by your fame, would have ascribed it to your benevolence, and America, intoxicated by the grant, would have slumbered in her fetters.

But this method of studying the progress of the passions, in order to ascertain the probable conduct of mankind, is a philosophy in politics which those who preside at St. James's have no conception of. They know no other influence than corruption, and reckon all their probabilities from precedent. A new case is to them a new world, and while they are seeking for a parallel they get lost. The talents of Lord Mansfield can be estimated at best no higher than those of a sophist. He understands the subtleties but not the elegance of nature; and by continually viewing mankind through the cold medium of the law, never thinks of penetrating into the warmer region of the mind. As for Lord North, it is his happiness to have in him more philosophy than sentiment, for he bears flogging like a top, and sleeps the better for it. His punishment becomes his support, for while he suffers the lash for his sins, he keeps himself up by twirling about. In politics, he is a good arithmetician, and in every thing else nothing at all.

There is one circumstance which comes so much within Lord North's province as a financier, that I am surprised it should escape him. which is, the different abilities of the two countries in supporting the expense; for, strange as it may seem, England is not a match for America in this particular. By a curious kind of revolution in accounts, the people of England seem to mistake their poverty for their riches; that is, they reckon their national debt as a part of their national wealth. They make the same kind of error which a man would do, who after mortgaging his estate, should add the money borrowed, to the full value of the estate, in order to count up his worth, and in this case he would conceive that he got rich by running into debt. Just thus it is with England. The government owed at the beginning of this war one hundred and thirty-five millions sterling, and though the individuals to whom it was due, had a right to reckon their shares as so much private property, yet to the nation collectively it was so much poverty. There is as effectual limits to public debts as to private ones, for when once the money borrowed is so great, as to require the whole yearly revenue to discharge the interest thereon, there is an end to further borrowing; in the same manner as when the interest of a man's debts amounts to the yearly income of his estate, there is an end to his credit. This is nearly the case with England, the interest of her present debt being at least equal to one-half of her yearly revenue, so that out of ten millions annually collected by taxes, she has but five that she can call her own.

The very reverseof this was the case with America; she began the war without any debt upon her, and it order to carry it on, she neither raised money by taxes nor borrowed it upon interest, but created it; and he situation at this time continues so much the reverse of yours that taxing would make her rich, whereas it would make you poor. When we shall have sunk the sumwhich we have created, we shall then be out of debt, be just as rich as when we began, and all the while we an doing it shall feel no difference, because the value will rise as the quantity decreases.

There was not a country in the world so capable of bearing the expense of a war as America; not only be cause she was not in debt when she began, but because the country is young and capable of infinite improvement, and has an almost boundless tract of new lands in store; whereas England has got to her extent of age and growth, and has no unoccupied land or property in reserve. The one is like a young heir coming to a large improvable estate; the other like an old man whose chances are over, and his estate mortgaged for half its worth.

In the second number of the *Crisis*, which I find has been republished in England, I endeavored to set forth the impracticability of conquering America. I stated every case that I conceived could possibly happen, and ventured to predict its consequences. As my conclusions were drawn not artfully, but naturally, they have all proved to be true. I was upon the spot; knew the politics of America, her strength and resources, and by a train of services, the best in my power to render, was honored with the friendship of the Congress, the army and the people. I considered the cause a just one. I know and feel it a just one, and under that confidence never made my own profit or loss an object. My endeavor was to have the matter well understood on both sides, and I conceived myself tendering a general service, by setting forth to the one the impossibility of being conquered, and to the other the impossibility of conquering. Most of the arguments made use of by the ministry for supporting the war, are the very arguments that ought to have been used against supporting it; and the plans by which they thought to conquer, are the very plans in which they were sure to be defeated. They have taken every thing up at the wrong end. Their ignorance is astonishing, and were you in my situation you would see it. They may, perhaps, have your confidence, but I am persuaded that they would make very indifferent members of Congress. I know what England is, and what America is, and from the compound of knowledge, am better enabled to judge of the issue than what the king or any of his ministers can be.

In this number I have endeavored to show the ill policy and disadvantages of the war. I believe many of my remarks are new. Those which are not so, I have studied to improve and place in a manner that may be clear and striking. Your failure is, I am persuaded, as certain as fate. America is above your reach. She is at least your equal in the world, and her independence neither rests upon your consent, nor can it be prevented by your arms. In short, you spend your substance in vain, and impoverish yourselves without a hope.

But suppose you had conquered America, what advantages, collectively or individually, as merchants, manufacturers, or conquerors, could you have looked for? This is an object you seemed never to have attended to. Listening for the sound of victory, and led away by the frenzy of arms, you neglected to reckon either the cost or the consequences. You must all pay towards the expense; the poorest among you must bear his share, and it is both your right and your duty to weigh seriously the matter. Had America been conquered, she might have been parceled out in grants to the favorites at court, but no share of it would have fallen to you. Your taxes would not have been lessened, because she would have been in no condition to have paid any towards your relief. We are rich by a contrivance of our own, which would have ceased as soon as you became masters. Our paper money will be of no use in England, and silver and gold we have none. In the last war you made many conquests, but were any of your taxes lessened thereby? On the contrary, were you not taxed to pay for the charge of making them, and have not the same been the case in every war?

To the parliament I wish to address myself in a more particular manner. They appear to have supposed themselves partners in the chase, and to have hunted with the lion from an expectation of a right in the booty; but in this it is most probable they would, as legislators, have been disappointed. The case is quite a new one, and many unforeseen difficulties would have arisen thereon. The parliament claimed a legislative right over America, and the war originated from that pretence. But the army is supposed to belong to the crown, and if America had been conquered through their means, the claim of

the legislature would have been suffocated in the conquest.
Ceded or conquered countries are supposed to be out of the
authority of parliament. Taxation is exercised over them by
prerogative and not by law. It was attempted to be done in the
Grenadas a few years ago, and the only reason why it was not
done was because the crown had made a prior relinquishment
of its claim. Therefore, parliament have been all this while
supporting measures for the establishment of their authority, in
the issue of which, they would have been triumphed over by
the prerogative. This might have opened anew and interesting
opposition between the parliament and the crown. The crown
would have said that it conquered for itself, and that to conquer for parliament was an unknown case. The parliament
might have replied, that America not being a foreign country,
but a country in rebellion, could not be said to be conquered,
but reduced; and thus continued their claim by disowning the
term. The crown might have rejoined, that however America
might be considered at first, she became foreign at last by a
declaration of independence, and a treaty with France; and that
her case being, by that treaty, put within the law of nations,
was out of the law of parliament. The parliament might have
maintained, that as their claim over America had never been
surrendered, so neither could it be taken away. The crown
might have insisted, that though the claim of parliament could
not be taken away, yet, being an inferior, it might be super-
seded; and that, whether the claim was withdrawn from the
object, or the object taken from the claim, the same separation
ensued; and that America being subdued after a treaty with
France, was to all intents and purposes a regal conquest, and
of course the sole property of the king. The parliament, as the
legal delegates of the people, might have contended against
the term "inferior," and rested the case upon the antiquity of

power, and this would have brought on a set of very interesting and rational questions.

First, What is the original fountain of power and honor in any country?

Secondly, Whether the prerogative does not belong to the people?

Thirdly, Whether there is any such thing as the English constitution?

Fourthly, Of what use is the crown to the people?

Fifthly, Whether he who invented a crown was not an enemy to mankind?

Sixthly, Whether it is not a shame for a man to spend a million a year and do no good for it, and whether the money might not be better applied?

Seventhly, Whether such a man is not better dead than alive?

Eighthly, Whether a congress, constituted like that of America, is not the most happy and consistent form of government in the world?—With a number of others of the same import.

In short, the contention about the dividend might have distracted the nation; for nothing is more common than to agree in the conquest and quarrel for the prize; therefore it is, perhaps, a happy circumstance, that our successes have prevented the dispute.

If the parliament had been thrown out in their claim, which it is most probable they would, the nation likewise would have been thrown out in their expectation; for as the taxes would have been laid on by the crown without the parliament, the revenue arising therefrom, if any could have arisen, would not have gone into the exchequer, but into the privy purse, and so far from lessening the taxes, would not even have been added to them, but served only as pocket money to the crown. The more I reflect on this matter, the more I am astonished at the blindness and ill policy of my countrymen, whose wisdom seems to operate without discernment, and their strength without an object.

To the great bulwark of the nation, I mean the mercantile and manufacturing part thereof, I likewise present my address. It is your interest to see America an independent country, and not a conquered one. If conquered, she is ruined; and if ruined, poor; consequently her trade will be a trifle, and her credit doubtful. If independent, she flourishes, and from her flourishing must your profits arise. It matters nothing to you who governs America, if your manufactures find a consumption there. Some articles will consequently be obtained from other places, and right they should; but the demand of others will increase, by the great influx of inhabitants which a state of independence and peace will occasion, and in the final event you may be enriched. The commerce of America is perfectly free, and ever will be so. She will consign away no part of it to any nation. She has not to her friends, and certainly will not to her enemies, though it is probable that your narrow-minded politicians, thinking to please you thereby, may some time or other unnecessarily make such a proposal. Trade flourishes best when it is free, and it is weak policy to attempt to fetter it. Her treaty with France is on the most liberal and generous principles, and the French, in their conduct towards her, have proved themselves to be philosophers, politicians, and gentlemen.

To the ministry I likewise address myself. You, gentlemen, have studied the ruin of your country, from which it is not within your abilities to rescue her. Your attempts to recover her are as ridiculous as your plans which involved her are detestable. The commissioners, being about to depart, will probably bring you this, and with it my sixth number, addressed to them; and in so doing they carry back more

Common Sense than they brought, and you likewise will have more than when you sent them.

Having thus addressed you severally, I conclude by addressing you collectively. It is a long lane that has no turning. A period of sixteen years of misconduct and misfortune, is certainly long enough for any one nation to suffer under; and upon a supposition that war is not declared between France and you, I beg to place a line of conduct before you that will easily lead you out of all your troubles. It has been hinted before, and cannot be too much attended to.

Suppose America had remained unknown to Europe till the present year, and that Mr. Banks and Dr. Solander, in another voyage round the world, had made the first discovery of her, in the same condition that she is now in, of arts, arms, numbers, and civilization. What, I ask, in that case, would have been your conduct towards her? For *that* will point out what it ought to be now. The problems and their solutions are equal, and the right line of the one is the parallel of the other. The question takes in every circumstance that can possibly arise. It reduces politics to a simple thought, and is moreover a mode of investigation, in which, while you are studying your interest, the simplicity of the case will cheat you into good temper. You have nothing to do but to suppose that you have found America, and she appears found to your hand, and while in the joy of your heart you stand still to admire her, the path of politics rises straight before you.

Were I disposed to paint a contrast, I could easily set off what you have done in the present case, against what you would have done in *that* case, and by justly opposing them, conclude a picture that would make you blush. But, as when any of the prouder passions are hurt, it is much better philosophy to let a man slip into a good temper than to attack him in a bad one; for that reason, therefore, I only state the case, and leave you to reflect upon it.

To go a little back into politics, it will be found that the true interest of Britain lay in proposing and promoting the independence of America immediately after the last peace; for the expense which Britain had then incurred by defending America as her own dominions, ought to have shown her the policy and necessity of changing the *style* of the country, as the best probable method of preventing future wars and expense, and the only method by which she could hold the commerce without the charge of sovereignty. Besides which, the title which she assumed, of parent country, led to, and pointed out the propriety, wisdom and advantage of a separation; for, as in private life, children grow into men, and by setting up for themselves, extend and secure the interest of the whole family, so in the settlement of colonies large enough to admit of maturity, the same policy should be pursued, and the same consequences would follow. Nothing hurts the affections both of parents and children so much, as living too closely connected, and keeping up the distinction too long. Domineering will not do over those, who, by a progress in life, have become equal in rank to their parents, that is, when they have families of their own; and though they may conceive themselves the subjects of their advice, will not suppose them the objects of their government. I do not, by drawing this parallel, mean to admit the title of *parent country*, because, if it is due any where, it is due to Europe collectively, and the first settlers from England were driven here by persecution. I mean only to introduce the term for the sake of policy and to show from your title the line of your interest.

When you saw the state of strength and opulence, and that by her own industry, which America had arrived at, you ought to have advised her to set up for herself, and proposed an alliance of interest with her, and in so doing you would have drawn, and that at her own expense, more real advantage, and more military supplies and assistance, both of ships and men, than from any weak and wrangling government you could exercise over her. In short, had you studied only the domestic politics of a family, you would have learned how to govern the state; but, instead of this easy and natural line, you flew out into every thing which was wild and outrageous, till, by following the passion and stupidity of the pilot, you wrecked the vessel within sight of the shore.

Having shown what you ought to have done, I now proceed to show why it was not done. The caterpillar circle of the court, had an interest to pursue, distinct from, and opposed to yours; for though by the independence of America and an alliance therewith, the trade would have continued, if not increased, as in many articles neither country can go to a better market, and though, by defending and protecting herself, she would have been no expense to you, and consequently your national charges would have decreased, and your taxes might have been proportionably lessened thereby; yet the striking off so many places from the court calendar was put in opposition to the interest of the nation.

The loss of thirteen government ships, with their appendages here and in England, is a shocking sound in the ear of a hungry courtier. Your present king and ministry will be the ruin of you; and you had better risk a revolution and call a congress, than be thus led on from madness to despair, and from despair to ruin. America has set you the example, and you may follow it and be free.

I now come to the last part, a war with France. This is what no man in his senses will advise you to, and all good men would wish to prevent. Whether France will declare war against you, is not for me in this place to mention, or to hint, even if I knew it; but it must be madness in you to do it first. The matter is come now to a full crisis, and peace is easy if willingly set about.

Whatever you may think, France has behaved handsomely to you. She would have been unjust to herself to have acted otherwise than she did; and having accepted our offer of alliance she gave you genteel notice of it. There was nothing in her conduct reserved or indelicate, and while she announced her determination to support her treaty, she left you to give the first offence.

America, on her part, has exhibited a character of firmness to the world. Unprepared and unarmed, without form or government, she singly opposed a nation that domineered over half the globe. The greatness of the deed demands respect; and although you may feel resentment, you are compelled both to wonder and admire.

Here I rest my arguments and finish my address. Such as it is, it is a gift, and you are welcome. It was always my design to dedicate a *Crisis* to you, when the time should come that would properly *make it a Crisis*; and when, likewise, I should catch myself in a temper to write it, and suppose you in a condition to read it. *That* time has now arrived, and with it the opportunity of conveyance. For the commissioners—*poor commissioners!* having proclaimed, that "*yet forty days and Nineveh shall be overthrown,*" have waited out the date, and, discontented with their God, are returning to their gourd. And all the harm I wish them is, that it may not *wither* about their ears, and that they may not make their exit in the belly of a whale.

COMMON SENSE.
Philadelphia, Nov. 21, 1778.

P. S. Though in the tranquillity of my mind I have concluded
with a laugh, yet I have something to mention to the *commissioners*, which, to them, is serious and worthy their
attention. Their authority is derived from an act of parliament, which likewise describes and *limits* their *official*
powers. Their commission, therefore, is only a recital, and
personal investiture of those powers, or a nomination and
description of the persons who are to execute them. Had it
contained any thing contrary to, or gone beyond the line of
the written law, from which it is derived, and by which it is
bound, it would, by the English constitution, have been
treason in the crown, and the king been subject to an
impeachment. He dared not, therefore, put in his commission what you have put in your proclamation, that is, he
dared not have authorized you in that commission to burn or
destroy any thing in America. You are both in the *act* and in
the *commission* styled *commissioners for restoring peace*,
and the methods for doing it are there pointed out. Your last
proclamation is signed by you as commissioners *under that
act*. You make parliament the patron of its contents. Yet, in
the body of it, you insert matters contrary both to the spirit
and letter of the act, and what likewise your king dared not
have put in his commission to you. The state of things in
England, gentlemen, is too ticklish for you to run hazards.
You are *accountable to parliament for the execution of that
act according to the letter of it*. Your heads may pay for
breaking it, for you certainly have broke it by exceeding it.
And as a friend, who would wish you to escape the paw of
the lion, as well as the belly of the whale, I civilly hint to
you, *to keep within compass*.

Sir Harry Clinton, strictly speaking, is as accountable as
the rest; for though a general, he is likewise a commissioner,
acting under a superior authority. His first obedience is due
to the act; and his plea of being a general, will not and

cannot clear him as a commissioner, for that would suppose the crown, in its single capacity, to have a power of dispensing with an act of parliament. Your situation, gentlemen, is nice and critical, and the more so because England is unsettled. Take heed! Remember the times of Charles the First! For Laud and Stafford fell by trusting to a hope like yours.

Having thus shown you the danger of your proclamation, I now show you the folly of it. The means contradict your design; you threaten to lay waste, in order to render America a useless acquisition of alliance to France. I reply, that the more destruction you commit (if you could do it) the more valuable to France you make that alliance. You can destroy only houses and goods; and by so doing you increase our demand upon her for materials and merchandise; for the wants of one nation, provided it has *freedom* and *credit*, naturally produces riches to the other; and, as you can neither ruin the land nor prevent the vegetation, you would increase the exportation of our produce in payment, which would be to her a fund of wealth. In short, had you cast about for a plan on purpose to enrich your enemies, you could not have hit upon a better. C. S.

THE CRISIS
NUMBER VIII

Addressed to the People of England

"TRUSTING (says the king of England in his speech of November last,) in the divine providence, and in the justice of my cause, I am firmly resolved to prosecute the war with vigor, and to make every exertion in order to compel our enemies to equitable terms of peace and accommodation." To this declaration the United States of America, and the confederated powers of Europe will reply, *if Britain will have war, she shall have enough of it.*

Five years have nearly elapsed since the commencement of hostilities, and every campaign, by a gradual decay, has lessened your ability to conquer, without producing a serious thought on your condition or your fate. Like a prodigal lingering in an habitual consumption, you feel the relics of life, and mistake them for recovery. New schemes, like new medicines, have administered fresh hopes, and prolonged the disease instead of curing it. A change of generals, like a change of physicians, served only to keep the flattery alive, and furnish new pretences for new extravagance.

*"Can Britain fail?"** has been proudly asked at the commencement of every enterprise, and that *"whatever she wills is fate,"*† has been given with the solemnity of prophetic confidence, and though the question has been constantly replied to

---

* Whitehead's New Year's Ode for 1776.

† Ode at the installation of Lord North, for Chancellor of the University of Oxford.

by disappointment, and the prediction falsified by misfortune, yet still the insult continued, and your catalogue of national evils increased therewith. Eager to persuade the world of her power, she considered destruction as the minister of greatness, and conceived that the glory of a nation like that of an Indian, lay in the number of its scalps and the miseries it inflicts.

Fire, sword and want, as far as the arms of Britain could extend them, have been spread with wanton cruelty along the coast of America; and while you, remote from the scene of suffering, had nothing to lose and as little to dread, the information reached you like a tale of antiquity, in which the distance of time defaces the conception, and changes the severest sorrows into convertable amusement.

This makes the second paper, addressed perhaps in vain, to the people of England. That advice should be taken wherever example has failed, or precept be regarded where warning is ridiculed, is like a picture of hope resting on despair: but when time shall stamp with universal currency, the facts you have long encountered with a laugh, and the irresistible evidence of accumulated losses, like the hand-writing on the wall, shall add terror to distress, you will then, in a conflict of sufferings, learn to sympathise with others by feeling for yourselves.

The triumphant appearance of the combined fleets in the channel and at your harbor's mouth, and the expedition of Captain Paul Jones, on the western and eastern coasts of England and Scotland, will, by placing you in the condition of an endangered country, read to you a stronger lecture on the calamities of invasion, and bring to your minds a truer picture of promiscuous distress, than the most finished rhetoric can describe or the keenest imagination conceive.

Hitherto you have experienced the expenses, but nothing of the miseries of war. Your disappointments have been accompanied with no immediate suffering, and your losses came to you only by intelligence. Like fire at a distance you heard not even the cry; you felt not the danger, you saw not the confusion. To you every thing has been foreign but the taxes to support it. You knew not what it was to be alarmed at midnight with an armed enemy in the streets. You were strangers to the distressing scene of a family in flight, and to the thousand restless cares and tender sorrows that incessantly arose. To see women and children wandering in the severity of winter, with the broken remains of a well furnished house, and seeking shelter in every crib and hut, were matters you had no conception of. You knew not what it was to stand by and see your goods chopped for fuel, and your beds ripped to pieces to make packages for plunder. The misery of others, like a tempestuous night, added to the pleasures of your own security. You even enjoyed the storm, by contemplating the difference of conditions, and that carried sorrow into the breasts of thousands, served but to heighten in you a species of tranquil pride.—Yet these are but the fainter sufferings of war, when compared with carnage and slaughter, the miseries of a military hospital, or a town in flames.

The people of America, by anticipating distress, had fortified their minds against every species you could inflict. They had resolved to abandon their homes, to resign them to destruction, and to seek new settlements rather than submit. Thus familiarized to misfortune, before it arrived, they bore their portion with the less regret: the justness of their cause was a continual source of consolation, and the hope of final victory, which never left them, served to lighten the load and sweeten the cup allotted them to drink.

But when their suffering shall become yours, and invasion be transferred upon the invaders, you will have neither their extended wilderness to fly to, their cause to comfort you, nor their hopes to rest upon. Distress with them was sharpened by no self-reflection. They had not brought it on themselves. On the contrary, they had by every proceeding endeavored to avoid it, and had descended even below the mark of congressional character, to prevent a war. The national honor or the advantages of independence were matters, which at the commencement of the dispute, they had never studied, and it was only at the last moment that the measure was resolved on. Thus circumstanced, they naturally and conscientiously felt a dependance upon providence. They had a clear pretension to it, and had they failed therein, infidelity had gained a triumph.

But your condition is the reverse of theirs. Everything you suffer you have sought; nay, had you created mischiefs on purpose to inherit them, you could not have secured your title by a firmer deed. The world awakens with no pity at your complaints. You felt none for others; you deserve none for yourselves. Nature does not interest herself in cases like yours, but on the contrary turns from them with dislike and abandons them to punishment. You may now present memorials to what court you please, but so far as America is the object, none will listen. The policy of Europe and the propensity there is in every mind to curb insulting ambition, and bring cruelty to judgment, are unitedly against you; and where nature and interest reinforce each other, the compact is too intimate to be dissolved.

Make but the case of others your own, and your own theirs, and you will then have a clear idea of the whole. Had France acted towards her colonies as you have done, you would have branded her with every epithet of abhorrence; and had you like her, stepped in to succor a struggling people, all Europe must have echoed with your own applause. But entangled in the passion of dispute, you see it not as you ought, and form opinions thereon which suit with no interest but your own. You wonder America does not rise in union with you to impose on herself a portion of your taxes and reduce herself to unconditional submission. You are amazed that the southern powers of Europe do not assist you in conquering a country which is afterwards to be turned against themselves; and that the northern ones do not contribute to reinstate you in America, who already enjoy the market for naval stores by the separation. You seem surprised that Holland does not pour in her succors, to maintain you mistress of the seas, when her own commerce is suffering by your act of navigation, or that any country should study her own interests while yours is on the carpet.

Such excesses of passionate folly, and unjust as well as unwise resentment, have driven you on, like Pharoah, to unpitied miseries, and while the importance of the quarrel shall perpetuate your disgrace, the flag of America will carry it around the world. The natural feelings of every rational being will be against you, and wherever the story shall be told, you will have neither excuse nor consolation left. With an unsparing hand and an insatiable mind, you have desolated the world, to gain dominion and to lose it; and while in a frenzy of avarice and ambition, the east and the west are doomed to tributary bondage, you rapidly earned destruction as the wages of a nation.

At the thoughts of a war at home every man amongst you ought to tremble. The prospect is far more dreadful there than in America. Here the party that was against the measures of the continent, were in general a kind of neutrals who added strength to neither army. There does not exist a being so devoid of sense and sentiment as to covet *"unconditional submission,"*

and therefore no man in America could be with you in principle. Several might, from a cowardice of mind, *prefer* it to the
hardships and dangers of *opposing* it; but the same disposition
that gave them such a choice, unfitted them to act either for or
against us. But England is rent into parties, with equal shares
of resolution. The principle which produced the war divides
the nation. Their animosities are in the highest state of fer-
mentation, and both sides, by a call of the militia, are in arms.
No human foresight can discern, no conclusion can be formed,
what turn a war might take, if once set on foot by an invasion.
She is not now in a fit position to make a common cause of her
own affairs, and having no conquests to hope for abroad, and
nothing but expenses arising at home, her everything is staked
upon a defensive combat, and the further she goes the worse
she is off.

There are situations a nation may be in, in which peace or
war, abstracted from every other consideration, may be politically right or wrong. When nothing can be lost by a war, but
what must be lost without it, war is then the policy of that
country; and such was the situation of America at the commencement of hostilities: but when no security can be gained
by a war, but what may be accomplished by a peace, the case
becomes reversed, and such now is the situation of England.

That America is beyond the reach of conquest, is a fact
which experience has shown and time confirmed, and this
admitted, what, I ask, is now the object of contention? If there
be any honor in pursuing self-destruction with inflexible passion—if national suicide be the perfection of national glory,
you may, with all the pride of criminal happiness, expire unen-
vied and unrivalled.—But when the tumult of war shall cease,
and the tempest of present passions be succeeded by calm
reflection, or when those who, surviving its fury, shall inherit

from you a legacy of debts and misfortunes, when the yearly revenue shall scarcely be able to discharge the interest of the one, and no possible remedy be left for the other: ideas, far different from the present, will arise and embitter the remembrance of former follies. A mind disarmed of its rage, feels no pleasure in contemplating a frantic quarrel. Sickness of thought, the sure consequence of conduct like yours, leaves no ability for enjoyment, no relish for resentment; and though, like a man in a fit, you feel not the injury of the struggle, nor distinguish between strength and disease, the weakness will nevertheless be proportioned to the violence, and the sense of pain increase with the recovery.

To what persons or to whose system of politics you owe your present state of wretchedness, is a matter of total indifference to America. They have contributed, however unwillingly, to set her above themselves, and she in the tranquillity of conquest resign the enquiry. The case now is not so properly who began the war, as who continues it. That there are men in all countries to whom a state of war is a mine of wealth, is a fact never to be doubted. Characters like these naturally breed in the putrefaction of distempered times, and after fattening on the disease, they perish with it, or impregnated with the stench, retreat into obscurity.

But there are several erroneous notions to which you likewise owe a share of your misfortunes, and which if continued will only increase your trouble and your losses. An opinion hangs about the gentlemen of the minority, that America would relish measures under *their* administration, which she would not from the present cabinet. On this rock Lord Chatham would have split had he gained the helm, and several of his survivors are steering the same course. Such distinctions in the infancy of the argument had some degree of foundation, but they now serve no other purpose than to lengthen out a war, in which the limits of a dispute, being fixed by the fate of arms, and guaranteed by treaties, are not to be changed or altered by trivial circumstances.

The ministry and many of the minority sacrifice their time in disputing on a question with which they have nothing to do, namely, whether America shall be independent or not? whereas the only question that can come under their determination is, whether they will accede to it or not? They confound a military question with a political one, and undertake to supply by a vote what they lost by a battle. Say, she shall not be independent, and it will signify as much as if they voted against a decree of fate, or say that she shall, and she will be no more independent than before. Questions which when determined cannot be executed, serve only to show the folly of dispute and the weakness of disputants.

From a long habit of calling America your own, you suppose her governed by the same prejudices and conceits which govern yourself. Because you have set up a particular denomination of religion to the exclusion of all others, you imagine she must do the same, and because you, with an unsociable narrowness of mind, have cherished enmity against France and Spain, you suppose her alliance must be defective in friendship. Copying her notions of the world from you, she formerly thought as you instructed, but now feeling herself free, and the prejudice removed, she thinks and acts upon a different system. It frequently happens that in proportion as we are taught to dislike persons and countries, not knowing why, we feel an ardor of esteem upon the removal of the mistake. It seems as if something was to be made amends for, and we eagerly give in to every office of friendship, to atone for the injury of the error.

But perhaps there is something in the extent of countries, which, among the generality of people, insensibly communicates extension of the mind. The soul of an islander in its native state seems bounded by the foggy confines of the water's edge, and all beyond affords to him matters only for profit or curiosity, not for friendship. His island is to him his world, and fixed to that, his every thing centres in it; while those who are inhabitants of a continent, by casting their eye over a larger field, take in likewise a larger intellectual circuit, and thus approaching nearer to an acquaintance with the universe, their atmosphere of thought is extended, and their liberality fills a wider space. In short, our minds seem to be measured by countries when we are men, as they are by places, when we are children, and until something happens to disentangle us from the prejudice, we serve under it without perceiving it.

In addition to this, it may be remarked, that men who study any universal science, the principles of which are universally known, or admitted, and applied without distinction to the common benefit of all countries, obtain thereby a larger share of philanthropy than those who only study national arts and improvements. Natural philosophy, mathematics and astronomy, carry the mind from the country to the creation, and give it a fitness suited to the extent. It was not Newton's honor, neither could it be his pride, that he was an Englishman, but that he was a philosopher The Heavens had liberated him from the prejudices of an island, and science had expanded his soul as boundless as his studies.

COMMON SENSE.
Philadelphia, March, 1780.

THE CRISIS
NUMBER IX

HAD America pursued her advantages with half the spirit that she resisted her misfortunes, she would, before now, have been a conquering and a peaceful people; but lulled in the lap of soft tranquilllity, she rested on her hopes, and adversity only has convulsed her into action. Whether subtlety or sincerity, at the close of the last year, induced the enemy to an appearance for peace, is a point not material to know: it is sufficient that we see the effects it has had on our politics, and that we sternly rise to resent the delusion.

The war, on the part of America, has been a war of natural feelings. Brave in distress; serene in conquest; drowsy while at rest; and in every situation generously disposed to peace. A dangerous calm, and a most heightened zeal, have, as circumstances varied, succeeded each other. Every passion, but that of despair, has been called to a tour of duty; and so mistaken has been the enemy, of our abilities and disposition that when she supposed us conquered, we rose the conquerors. The extensiveness of the United States, and the variety of their resources; the universality of their cause, the quick operation of their feelings, and the similarity of their sentiments, have, in every trying situation, produced a *something*, which, favored by Providence, and pursued with ardor, has accomplished in an instant the business of a campaign. We have never deliberately sought victory, but snatched it; and bravely undone in an hour, the blotted operations of a season.

The reported fate of Charleston, like the misfortunes of 1776, has at last called forth a spirit, and kindled up a flame, which perhaps no other event could have produced. If the enemy has circulated a falsehood, they have unwisely aggravated us into life, and if they have told us a truth, they have unintentionally done us a service. We were returning with folded arms from the fatigues of war, and thinking and sitting leisurely down to enjoy repose. The dependence that has been put upon Charleston threw a drowsiness over America. We looked on the business done—the conflict over—the matter settled—or that all which remained unfinished would follow of itself. In this state of dangerous relaxation, exposed to the poisonous infusions of the enemy, and having no common danger to attract our attention, we were extinguishing by stages the ardor we began with, and surrendering by piecemeal the virtue that defended us.

Afflicting as the loss of Charleston may be, yet if it universally rouse us from the slumber of twelve months past, and renew in us the spirit of former days, it will produce an advantage more important than its loss. America ever *is* what she *thinks* herself to be. Governed by sentiment and acting her own mind, she becomes as she pleases, the victor or the victim.

It is not the conquest of towns, nor the accidental capture of garrisons, that can reduce a country so extensive as this. The sufferings of one part can never be relieved by the exertions of another, and there is no situation the enemy can be placed in, that does not afford to us the same advantages he seeks himself. By dividing his force, he leaves every post attackable. It is a mode of war that carries with it a confession of weakness, and goes on the principle of distress, rather than conquest.

The decline of the enemy is visible, not only in their operations, but in their plans; Charleston originally made but a secondary object in the system of attack, and it is now become their principal one, because they have not been able to succeed elsewhere. It would have carried a cowardly appearance in Europe had they formed their grand expedition in 1776, against a part of the continent where there was no army, or not a sufficient one to oppose them; but failing year after year in their impressions here, and to the eastward and northward, they deserted their first capital design, and prudently contenting themselves with what they can get, give a flourish of honor to conceal disgrace.

But this piecemeal work is not conquering the continent. It is a discredit in them to attempt it, and in us to suffer it. It is now full time to put an end to a war of aggravations, which, on one side, has no possible object, and on the other, has every inducement which honor, interest, safety and happiness, can inspire. If we suffer them much longer to remain among us, we shall become as bad as themselves. An association of vices will reduce us more than the sword. A nation hardened in the practice of iniquity knows better how to profit by it, than a young country newly corrupted. We are not a match for them in the line of advantageous guilt, nor they to us on the principles which we bravely set out with. Our first days were our days of honor. They have marked the character of America wherever the story of her wars are told; and convinced of this, we have nothing to do but wisely and unitedly to tread the well known track. The progress of a war is often as ruinous to individuals, as the issue of it is to a nation; and it is not only necessary that our forces be such that we be conquerors in the end, but that by timely exertions we be secure in the interim. The present campaign will afford an opportunity which has never presented itself before, and the preparations for it are equally necessary, whether Charleston stand or fall. Suppose the first, it is in that case only a failure of the enemy, not a defeat. All the conquest that a besieged town can hope for, is, not to be conquered; and compelling an enemy to raise the siege, is to the besieged a victory. But there must be a probability amounting almost to certainty, that would justify a garrison marching out to attack a retreat. Therefore should Charleston not be taken, and the enemy abandon the siege, every other part of the continent should prepare to meet them; and, on the contrary, should it be taken, the same preparations are necessary to balance the loss, and put ourselves in a condition to co-operate with our allies, immediately on their arrival.

We are not now fighting our battles alone, as we were in 1776; England, from a malicious disposition to America, has not, only not declared war against France and Spain, but the better to prosecute her passions here, has afforded those powers no military object, and avoids them to distress us. She will suffer her West India islands to be overrun by France, and her southern settlements to be taken by Spain, rather than quit the object that gratifies her revenge. This conduct, on the part of Britain, has pointed out the propriety of France sending a naval and land force to co-operate with America on the spot. Their arrival cannot be very distant, nor the ravages of the enemy long. In the mean time the part necessary to us needs no illustration. The recruiting the army, and procuring the supplies, are the two things most necessary to be accomplished, and a capture of either of the enemy's divisions will restore to America peace and plenty.

At a crisis, big, like the present, with expectation and events, the whole country is called to unanimity and exertion. Not an ability ought now to sleep that can produce but a mite to the general good, nor even a whisper to pass that militates against it. The necessity of the case, and the importance of the consequences, admit no delay from a friend—no apology from an enemy. To spare now, would be the height of extravagance, and to consult present ease, would be to sacrifice it, perhaps forever.

America, rich in patriotism and produce, can want neither

men nor supplies, when a serious necessity calls them forth. The slow operation of taxes, owing to the extensiveness of collection, and their depreciated value before they arrive in the treasury, have, in many instances, thrown a burden upon government, which has been artfully interpreted by the enemy into a general decline throughout the country. Yet this, inconvenient as it may at first appear, is not only remediable, but may be turned to an immediate advantage; for it makes no real difference, whether a certain number of men, or company of militia, (and in this country every man is a militia-man), are directed by law to send a recruit at their own expense, or whether a tax is laid on them for that purpose, and the man hired by government afterwards. The first, if there is any difference, is both cheapest and best, because it saves the expense which would attend collecting it as a tax, and brings a man sooner into the field than the modes of recruiting formerly used; and, on this principle, a law has been passed in this state, for recruiting two men from each company of militia, which will add upwards of a thousand to the force of the country.

But the flame which has broke forth in this city since the report from New York, of the loss of Charleston, not only does honor to the place, but like the blaze of 1776, will kindle into action the scattered sparks throughout America. The valor of a country may be learned by the bravery of its soldiery, and the general cast of its inhabitants, but confidence of success is best discovered by the active measures pursued by men of property; and when the spirit of enterprise becomes so universal as to act at once on all ranks of men, a war may then, and not till then, be styled truly popular.

In 1776, the ardor of the enterprising part was considerably checked by the real revolt of some, and the coolness of others. But in the present ease, there is a firmness in thesubstance and property of the country to the public cause. An association has been entered into by the merchants, tradesmen, and principal inhabitants of the city, to receive and support the new state money at the value of gold and silver; a measure which, while it does them honor, will likewise contribute to their interest, by rendering the operations of the campaign convenient and effectual.

Nor has the spirit of exertion stopped here. A voluntary subscription is likewise begun, to raise a fund of hard money, to be given as bounties, to fill up the full quota of the Pennsylvania line. It has been the remark of the enemy, that every thing in America has been done by the force of government; but when she sees individuals throwing in their voluntary aid, and facilitating the public measures in concert with the established powers of the country, it will convince her that the cause of America stands not on the will of a few, but on the broad foundation of property and popularity.

Thus aided and thus supported, disaffection will decline, and the withered head of tyranny expire in America. The ravages of the enemy will be short and limited, and like all their former ones, will produce a victory over themselves.

COMMON SENSE.
Philadelphia, June 9, 1780.

Note: At the time of writing this number of the *Crisis*, the loss of Charleston, though believed by some, was more confidently disbelieved by others. But there ought to be no longer a doubt upon the matter. Charleston is gone, and I believe for the want of a sufficient supply of provisions. The man that does not now feel for the honor of the best and noblest cause that ever a country engaged in, and exert himself accordingly, is no longer worthy of a peaceable residence among a people determined to be free.   C. S.

THE CRISIS
NUMBER X

On the Subject of Taxation

IT is impossible to sit down and think seriously on the affairs of America, but the original principles on which she resisted, and the glow and ardor they inspired, will occur like the undefaced remembrance of a lovely scene. To trace over in imagination the purity of the cause, the voluntary sacrifices made to support it, and all the various turnings of the war in its defence, is at once both paying and receiving respect. The principles deserve to be remembered, and to remember them rightly is repossessing them. In this indulgence of generous recollection we become gainers by what we seem to give, and the more we bestow the richer we become.

So extensively right was the ground on which America proceeded, that it not only took in every just and liberal sentiment which could impress the heart, but made it the direct interest of every class and order of men to defend the country. The war, on the part of Britain, was originally a war of covetousness. The sordid, and not the splendid passions gave it being. The fertile fields and prosperous infancy of America appeared to her as mines for tributary wealth. She viewed the hive, and disregarding the industry that had enriched it, thirsted for the honey. But in the present stage of her affairs, the violence of temper is added to the rage of avarice; and therefore, that which at the first setting out proceeded from purity of principle and public interest, is now heightened by all the obligations of necessity; for it requires but little knowledge of human nature to discern what would be the consequence, were America again reduced to the subjection of Britain. Uncontrolled power, in the hands of an incensed, imperious and rapacious conqueror, is an engine of dreadful execution, and woe be to that country over which it can be exercised. The names of whig and tory would then be sunk in the general term of rebel, and the oppression, whatever it might be, would, with very few instances of exception, light equally on all.

Britain did not go to war with America for the sake of dominion, because she was then in possession; neither was it for the extension of trade and commerce, because she had monopolized the whole, and the country had yielded to it; neither was it to extinguish what she might call rebellion, because before she began no resistance existed. It could then be from no other motive than avarice, or a design of establishing, in the first instance, the same taxes in America as are paid in England (which, as I shall presently show, are above eleven times heavier than the taxes we now pay for the present year, 1780) or, in the second instance, to confiscate the whole property of America, in case of resistance and conquest of the latter, of which she had then no doubt.

I shall now proceed to show what the taxes in England are, and what the yearly expense of the present war is to her—what the taxes of this country amount to, and what the annual expense of defending it effectually will be to us; and shall endeavor concisely to point out the cause of our difficulties, and the advantages on one side, and the consequences on the other, in case we do, or do not, put ourselves in an effectual state of defence. I mean to be open, candid, and sincere. I see a universal wish to expel the enemy from the country, a murmuring because the war is not carried on with more vigor, and my intention is to show, as shortly as possible, both the reason and the remedy.

The number of souls in England (exclusive of Scotland and Ireland) is seven millions,* and the number of souls in America is three millions.

The amount of taxes in England (exclusive of Scotland and Ireland) was, before the present war commenced, eleven millions six hundred and forty-two thousand six hundred and fifty-three pounds sterling; which, on an average, is no less a sum than one pound thirteen shillings and three-pence sterling per head per annum, men, women and children; besides county taxes, taxes for the support of the poor, and a tenth of all the produce of the earth for the support of the bishops and clergy.†

---

* This is taking the highest number that the people of England have been, or can be rated at.

† The following is taken from Dr. Price's state of the taxes of England, pages, 96, 97, 98. An account of the money drawn from the public by taxes, annually, being the medium of three years before the year 1776.

Amount of customs in England,	£2,528,275
Amount of the excise in England,	4,649,892
Land tax at 3s.	1,300,000
Land tax at 1s. in the pound,	450,000
Salt duties,	218,739
Duties on stamps, cards, dice, advertisements, bonds, leases, indentures, newspapers, almanacs, &c.	280,788
Duties on houses and windows,	385,369
Post office, seizures, wine licenses, hackney coaches, &c.	250,000
Annual profits from lotteries,	150,000
Expense of collecting the excise in England,	297,887
Expense of collecting the customs in England,	468,700
Interest of loans on the land tax at 4s. expenses of collection, militia, &c.	250,000
Perquisites, &c., to custom-house officers, &c., supposed	250,000
Expense of collecting the salt duties in England, 10½ per cent.	27,000
Bounties on fish exported,	18,000
Expense of collecting the duties on stamps, advertisements, &c., at 5¼ per cent.	18,000
Total	£11,642,653

Nearly five millions of this sum went annually to pay the interest of the national debt, contracted by former wars, and the remaining sum of six millions six hundred and forty-two thousand six hundred pounds was applied to defray the yearly expense of government, the peace establishment of the army and navy, placemen, pensioners, &c., consequently the whole of the enormous taxes being thus appropriated, she had nothing to spare out of them towards defraying the expenses of the present war or any other. Yet had she not been in debt at the beginning of the war, as we were not, and like us had only a land and not a naval war to carry on, her then revenue of eleven millions and a half pounds sterling would have defrayed all her annual expenses of war and government within each year.

But this not being the case with her, she is obliged to borrow about ten million pounds sterling yearly, to prosecute the war she is now engaged in, (this year she borrowed twelve,) and lay on new taxes to discharge the interest; and allowing that the present war has cost her only fifty millions sterling, the interest thereon, at five per cent., will be two millions and an half: therefore the amount of her taxes now must be fourteen millions, which on an average is no less than forty shillings sterling, per head, men, women and children, throughout the nation. Now as this expense of fifty millions was borrowed on the hopes of conquering America, and as it was avarice which first induced her to commence the war, how truly wretched and deplorable would the condition of this country be, were she, by her own remissness, to suffer an enemy of such a disposition, and so circumstanced, to reduce her to subjection.

I now proceed to the revenues of America.

I have already stated the number of souls in America to be three millions, and by a calculation that I have made, which I have every reason to believe is sufficiently correct, the whole expense of the war, and the support of the several governments, may be defrayed for two million pounds sterling annually; which, on an average, is thirteen shillings and four pence per head, men, women, and children, and the peace establishment at the end of the war, will be but three quarters of a million, or five shillings sterling per head. Now, throwing out of the question every thing of honor, principle, happiness, freedom and reputation in the world, and taking it up on the simple ground of interest, I put the following case:

Suppose Britain was to conquer America, and, as a conqueror, was to lay her under no other conditions than to pay the same proportion towards her annual revenue which the people of England pay; our share, in that case, would be six million pounds sterling yearly; can it then be a question, whether it is best to raise two millions to defend the country, and govern it ourselves, and only three quarters of a million afterwards, or pay six millions to have it conquered, and let the enemy govern it?

Can it be supposed that conquerors would choose to put themselves in a worse condition than what they granted to the conquered? In England, the tax on rum is five shillings and one penny sterling per gallon, which is one silver dollar and fourteen coppers. Now would it not be laughable to imagine, that after the expense they have been at, they would let either whig or tory drink it cheaper than themselves? Coffee, which is so considerable an article of consumption and support here, is there loaded with a duty, which makes the price between five and six shillings sterling per pound, and a penalty of fifty pounds sterling on any person detected in roasting it in his own house. There is scarcely a necessary of life that you can eat, drink, wear, or enjoy, that is not there loaded with a tax; even the light from heaven is only permitted to shine into their dwellings by paying eighteen pence sterling per window annually; and the humblest drink of life, small beer, cannot there be purchased without a tax of nearly two coppers per gallon, besides a heavy tax upon the malt, and another on the hops before it is brewed, exclusive of a land-tax on the earth which produces them. In short, the condition of that country, in point of taxation, is so oppressive, the number of her poor so great, and the extravagance and rapaciousness of the court so enormous, that, were they to effect a conquest of America, it is then only that the distresses of America would begin. Neither would it signify any thing to a man whether he be whig or tory. The people of England, and the ministry of that country, know us by no such distinctions. What they want is clear, solid revenue, and the modes which they would take to procure it, would operate alike on all. Their manner of reasoning would be short, because they would naturally infer that, if we were able to carry on a war of five or six years against them, we were able to pay the same taxes which they do.

I have already stated that the expense of conducting the present war, and the government of the several states, may be done for two millions sterling, and the establishment in the time of peace, for three quarters of a million.*

As to navy matters, they flourish so well, and are so well attended to by individuals, that I think it consistent on every principle of real use and economy, to turn the navy into hard money (keeping only three or four packets) and apply it to the service of the army. We shall not have a ship the less; the use

---

*I have made the calculations in sterling, because it is a rate generally known in all the states, and because, likewise, it admits of an easy comparison between our expenses to support the war, and those of the enemy. Four silver dollars and a half is one pound sterling, and three pence over.

of them, and the benefit from them, will be greatly increased, and their expense saved. We are now allied with a formidable naval power, from whom we derive the assistance of a navy. And the line in which we can prosecute the war, so as to reduce the common enemy and benefit the alliance most effectually, will be by attending closely to the land service.

I estimate the charge of keeping up and maintaining an army, officering them, and all expenses included, sufficient for the defence of the country, to be equal to the expense of forty thousand men at thirty pounds sterling per head, which is one million two hundred thousand pounds.

I likewise allow four hundred thousand pounds for continental expenses at home and abroad.

And four hundred thousand pounds for the support of the several state governments—the amount will then be,

For the army	£1,200,000
Continental expenses at home and abroad	400,000
Government of the several states	400,000
Total	£2,000,000

I take the proportion of this state, Pennsylvania, to be an eighth part of the thirteen United States; the quota then for us to raise will be two hundred and fifty thousand pounds sterling; two hundred thousand of which will be our share for the support and pay of the army, and continental expenses at home and abroad, and fifty thousand pounds for the support of the state government.

In order to gain an idea of the porportion in which the raising such a sum will fall, I make the following calculation.

Pennsylvania contains three hundred and seventy-five

thousand inhabitants, men, women and children; which is likewise an eighth of the number of inhabitants of the whole United States: therefore, two hundred and fifty thousand pounds sterling to be raised among three hundred and seventy-five thousand persons, is, on an average, thirteen shillings and four pence per head, per annum, or something more than one shilling sterling per month. And our proportion of three quarters of a million for the government of the country, in time of peace, will be ninety-three thousand seven hundred and fifty pounds sterling; fifty thousand of which will be for the government expenses of the state, and forty-three thousand seven hundred and fifty pounds for continental expenses at home and abroad.

The peace establishment then will, on an average, be five shillings sterling per head. Whereas, was England now to stop, and the war cease, her peace establishment would continue the same as it is now, viz., forty shillings per head; therefore was our taxes necessary for carrying on the war as much per head as hers now is, and the difference to be only whether we should, at the end of the war, pay at the rate of five shillings per head, or forty shillings per head, the case needs no thinking of. But as we can securely defend and keep the country for one-third less than what our burden would be if it was conquered, and support the governments afterward for one-eighth of what Britain would levy on us, and could I find a miser whose heart never felt the emotion of a spark of principle, even that man, uninfluenced by every love but the love of money, and capable of no attachment but to his interest, would and must, from the frugality which governs him, contribute to the defence of the country, or he ceases to be a miser and becomes an idiot. But when we take in with it every thing that can ornament mankind; when the line of our interest becomes the line of our happiness: when all that can cheer and animate the heart; when a sense of honor, fame, character, at home and abroad, are interwoven not only with the security but the increase of property, there exists not a man in America, unless he be an hired emissary, who does not see that his good is connected with keeping up a sufficient defence.

I do not imagine that an instance can be produced in the world, of a country putting herself to such an amazing charge to conquer and enslave another, as Britain has done. The sum is too great for her to think of with any tolerable degree of temper; and when we consider the burden she sustains, as well as the disposition she has shown, it would be the height of folly in us to suppose that she would not reimburse herself by the most rapid means, had she America once more within her power. With such an oppression of expense, what would an empty conquest be to her! What relief under such circumstances could she derive from a victory without a prize? It was money—it was revenue she first went to war for, and nothing but *that* would satisfy her. It is not the nature of avarice to be satisfied with any thing else. Every passion that acts upon mankind has a peculiar mode of operation. Many of them are temporary and fluctuating; they admit of cessation and variety. But avarice is a fixed, uniform passion. It neither abates of its vigor nor changes its object; and the reason why it does not, is founded in the nature of things, for wealth has not a rival where avarice is a ruling passion. One beauty may excel another, and extinguish from the mind of a man the pictured remembrance of a former one: but wealth is the phoenix of avarice, and therefore cannot seek a new object, because there is not another in the world.

I now pass on to show the value of the present taxes, and compare them with the annual expense; but this I shall preface with a few explanatory remarks.

There are two distinct things which make the payment of

taxes difficult; the one is the large and real value of the sum to be paid, and the other is the scarcity of the thing in which the payment is to be made; and although these appear to be one and the same, they are in several instances not only different, but the difficulty springs from different causes.

Suppose a tax was to be laid equal to one-half of what a man's yearly income is, such a tax could not be paid, because the property could not be spared; and on the other hand, suppose a very trifling tax was laid, to be collected in *pearls*, such a tax likewise could not be paid, because they could not be had. Now any person may see that these are distinct cases, and the latter of them is a representation of our own.

That the difficulty cannot proceed from the former, that is, from the real value or weight of the tax, is evident at the first view to any person who will consider it.

The amount of the quota of taxes for the state, for the present year, 1780, (and so in proportion for every other state), is twenty millions of dollars, which, at seventy for one, is but sixty-four thousand two hundred and eighty pounds three shillings sterling, and on an average, is no more than three shillings and five pence sterling per head, per annum, per man, woman and child, or three pence two-fifths per head per month. Now here is a clear, positive fact, that cannot be contradicted, and which proves that the difficulty cannot be in the weight of the tax, for in itself it is a trifle, and far from being adequate to our quota of the expense of the war. The quitrents of one penny sterling per acre on only one-half of the state, come to upwards of fifty thousand pounds, which is almost as much as all the taxes of the present year, and as those quit-rents made no part of the taxes then paid, and are now discontinued, the quantity of money drawn for public service this year, exclusive of the militia fines, which I shall take notice of in the process of this work, is less than what was paid and payable in any year preceding the revolution, and since the last war: what I mean is, that the quit-rents and taxes taken together came to a larger sum then, than the present taxes without the quit-rents do now.

My intention by these arguments and calculations is to place the difficulty to the right cause, and show that it does not proceed from the weight or worth of the tax; but from the scarcity of the medium in which it is paid; and to illustrate this point still further, I shall now show, that if the tax of twenty millions of dollars was of four times the value it now is, or nearly so, which would be about two hundred and fifty thousand pounds sterling, and would be our full quota, this sum would have been raised with more ease, and have been less felt, than the present sum of only sixty-four thousand two hundred and eighty pounds.

The convenience or inconvenience of paying a tax in money arises from the quantity of money that can be spared out of trade.

When the emissions stopped, the continent was left in possession of two hundred millions of dollars, perhaps as equally dispersed as it was possible for trade to do it. And as no more was to be issued, the rise or fall of prices could neither increase nor diminish the quantity. It therefore remained the same through all the fluctuations of trade and exchange.

Now had the exchange stood at twenty for one, which was the rate congress calculated upon when they arranged the quota of the several states the latter end of last year, trade would have been carried on for nearly four times less money than it is now, and consequently the twenty millions would have been spared with much greater ease, and when collected would have been of almost four times the value that they now are. And on the other hand, was the depreciation to be ninety or one hundred for one, the quantity required for trade would be more than at sixty or seventy for one, and though the value of them would be less, the difficulty of sparing the money out of trade would be greater. And on these facts and arguments I rest the matter, to prove that it is not the want of property, but the scarcity of the medium by which the proportion of property for taxation is to be measured out, that makes the embarassment which we lie under. There is not money enough, and, what is equally as true, the people will not let there be money enough.

While I am on the subject of the currency, I shall offer one remark which will appear true to every body, and can be accounted for by nobody, which is, that the better the times were, the worse the money grew; and the worse the times were, the better the money stood. It never depreciated by any advantage obtained by the enemy. The troubles of 1776, and the loss of Philadelphia in 1777, made no sensible impression on it, and every one knows that the surrender of Charleston did not produce the least alteration in the rate of exchange, which, for long before, and for more than three months after, stood at sixty for one. It seems as if the certainty of its being our own, made us careless of its value, and that the most distant thoughts of losing it made us hug it the closer, like something we were loth to part with; or that we depreciate it for our pastime, which, when called to seriousness by the enemy, we leave off to renew again at our leisure. In short, our good luck seems to break us, and our bad makes us whole.

Passing on from this digression, I shall now endeavor to bring into one view the several parts which I have already stated, and form thereon some propositions, and conclude.

I have placed before the reader, the average tax per head, paid by the people of England; which is forty shillings sterling.

And I have shown the rate on an average per head, which

will defray all the expenses of the war to us, and support the several governments without running the the country into debt, which is thirteen shillings and four pence. I have shown what the peace establishment may be conducted for, viz., an eighth part of what it would be if under the government of Britain.

And I have likewise shown what the average per head of the present taxes are, namely, three shillings and five-pence sterling, or three pence two-fifths per month; and that their whole yearly value, in sterling, is only sixty-four thousand two hundred and eighty pounds. Whereas our quota, to keep the payments equal with the expenses, is two hundred and fifty thousand pounds. Consequently, there is a deficiency of one hundred and eighty-five thousand seven hundred and twenty pounds, and the same proportion of defect, according to the several quotas, happens in every other state. And this defect is the cause why the army has been so indifferently fed, clothed and paid. It is the cause, likewise, of the nerveless state of the campaign, and the insecurity of the country. Now, if a tax equal to thirteen and four pence per head, will remove all these difficulties, make people secure in their homes, leave them to follow the business of their stores and farms unmolested, and not only keep out, but drive out the enemy from the country; and if the neglect of raising this sum will let them in, and produce the evils which might be prevented—on which side, I ask, does the wisdom, interest and policy lie? Or, rather, would it not be an insult to reason, to put the question? The sum when proportioned out according to the several abilities of the people, can hurt no one, but an inroad from the enemy ruins hundreds of families.

Look at the destruction done in this city. The many houses totally destroyed, and others damaged; the waste of fences in the country round it, besides the plunder of furniture, forage and provision. I do not suppose that half a million sterling would reinstate the sufferers; and, does this, I ask, bear any proportion to the expense that would make us secure. The damage, on an average, is at least ten pounds sterling per head, which is as much as thirteen shillings and four pence per head comes to for fifteen years. The same has happened on the frontiers, and in the Jerseys, New York, and other places where the enemy has been—Carolina and Georgia are likewise suffering the same fate.

That the people generally do not understand the insufficiency of the taxes to carry on the war, is evident, not only from common observation, but from the construction of several petitions, which were presented to the assembly of this state, against the recommendation of congress of the 18th of March last, for taking up and funding the present currency at forty for one, and issuing new money in its stead. The prayer of the petition was, *that the currency might be appreciated by taxes* (meaning the present taxes) *and that part of the taxes be applied to the support of the army, if the army could not be otherwise supported.* Now it could not have been possible for such a petition to have been presented, had the petitioners known that, so far from *part* of the taxes being sufficient for the support of the army, the *whole* of them falls three-fourths short of the year's expenses.

Before I proceed to propose methods by which a sufficiency of money may be raised, I shall take a short view of the general state of the country.

Notwithstanding the weight of the war, the ravages of the enemy, and the obstructions she has thrown in the way of trade and commerce, so soon does a young country outgrow misfortune, that America has already surmounted many that heavily oppressed her. For the first year or two of the war, we were shut up within our ports, scarce venturing to look towards the ocean. Now our rivers are beautified with large and valuable vessels, our stores filled with merchandise, and the produce of the country has a ready market, at an advantageous price. Gold and silver, that for a while seemed to have retreated again within the bowels of the earth, have once more risen into circulation, and every day adds new strength to trade, commerce and agriculture.

In a pamphlet, written by Sir John Dalrymple, and dispersed in America, in the year 1775, he asserted, that, *"two twenty-gun ships, nay,"* says he, *"tenders of those ships, stationed between Albemarle Sound and Chesapeake Bay, would shut up the trade of America for six hundred miles."*

How little did Sir John Dalrymple know of the abilities of America!

While under the government of Britain, the trade of this country was loaded with restrictions. It was only a few foreign ports which we were allowed to sail to. Now it is otherwise; and allowing that the quantity of trade is but half what it was before the war, the case must show the vast advantage of an open trade, because the present quantity under her restrictions could not support itself; from which I infer, that if half the quantity without the restrictions can bear itself up nearly, if not quite as well, as the whole when subject to them, how prosperous must the condition of America be when the whole shall return open with all the world. By the trade I do not mean the employment of a merchant only, but the whole interest and business of the country taken collectively.

It is not so much my intention, by this publication, to propose particular plans for raising money, as it is to show the necessity and the advantages to be derived from it. My principal design is, from the disposition of the people to the measures which I am fully persuaded it is their interest and duty to adopt, and which needs no other force to accomplish them than the force of being felt. But as every hint may be useful, I shall throw out a sketch, and leave others to make such improvements upon it as to them may appear reasonable.

The annual sum wanted is two millions, and the average rate in which it falls, is thirteen shillings and four pence per head.

Suppose, then, that we raise half the sum and sixty thousand pounds over. The average rate thereof will be seven shillings per head.

In this case we shall have half the supply that we want, and an annual fund of sixty thousand pounds whereon to borrow the other million; because sixty thousand pounds is the interest of a million at six per cent.; and if at the end of another year we should be obliged, by the continuance of the war, to borrow another million, the taxes will be increased to seven shillings and six pence; and thus for every million borrowed, an additional tax, equal to six pence per head, must be levied.

The sum to be raised next year will be one million and sixty thousand pounds: one-half of which I would propose should be raised by duties on imported goods, and the other by a tax on landed property and houses, or such other means as such state may devise.

But as the duties on imports and prize goods must be the same in all the states, therefore the rate per cent., or what other form the duty shall be laid, must be ascertained and regulated by Congress, and ingrafted in that form into the law of each state; and the monies arising therefrom carried into the treasury of each state. The duties to be paid in gold or silver.

There are many reasons why a duty on imports is the most convenient duty or tax that can be collected; one of which is, because the whole is payable in a few places in a country, and it likewise operates with the greatest ease and equality, because as every one pays in proportion to what they can afford, and therefore the tax is regulated by the abilities which every man supposes himself to have; or in other words, every man becomes his own assessor, and pays by a little at a time, when it suits him to buy. Besides, it is a tax which people may pay or let alone by not consuming the articles; and though the alternative may have no influence on their conduct, the power of choosing is an agreeable thing to the mind.

For my own part, it would be a satisfaction to me, was there a duty on all sorts of liquors during the war, as in my idea of things it would be an addition to the pleasures of society, to know, that when the health of the army goes round, a few drops from every glass becomes theirs. How often have I heard an emphatical wish, almost accompanied with a tear, *"Oh, that our poor fellows in the field had some of this!"* Why then need we suffer under a fruitless sympathy, when there is a way to enjoy both the wish and the entertainment at once?

But the great national policy of putting a duty upon imports is, that it either keeps the foreign trade in our own hands, or draws something for the defence of the country from every foreigner who participates in it with us.

Thus much for the first half of the taxes, and as each state will best devise means to raise the other half, I shall confine my remarks to the resources of this state.

The quota, then, of this state, of one million and sixty thousand pounds, will be one hundred and thirty-three thousand two hundred and fifty pounds, the half of which is sixty-six thousand six hundred and twenty-five pounds; and supposing one-fourth part of Pennsylvania inhabited, then a tax of one bushel of wheat on every twenty acres of land, one with another, would produce the sum, and all the present taxes to cease. Whereas, tithes of the bishops and clergy in England, exclusive of the taxes, are upwards of half a bushel of wheat on *every single* acre of land, good and bad, throughout the nation.

In the former part of this paper, I mentioned the militia fines, but reserved speaking to the matter, which I shall now do. The ground I shall put it upon is, that two millions sterling a year will support a sufficient army, and all the expenses of war and government, without having recourse to the inconvenient method of continually calling men from their employments, which, of all others, is the most expensive and the least substantial.

I consider the revenues created by taxes as the first and principal thing, and fines only as secondary and accidental things. It was not the intention of the militia law to apply the fines to any thing else but the support of the militia, neither do they produce any revenue to the state, yet these fines amount to more than all the taxes: for taking the muster-roll to be sixty thousand men, the fine on forty thousand who may not attend, will be sixty thousand pounds sterling, and those who muster, will give up a portion of time equal to half that sum, and if the eight classes should be called within the year, and one-third turn out, the fine on the remaining forty thousand would amount to seventy-two millions of dollars, besides the fifteen shillings on every hundred pounds of property, and the charge of seven and a half per cent., for collecting, in certain instances, which, on the whole, would be upwards of two hundred and fifty thousand pounds sterling.

Now if those very fines disable the country from raising a sufficient revenue without producing an equivalent advantage, would it not be for the ease and interest of all parties to increase the revenue, in the manner I have proposed, or any better, if a better can be devised, and cease the operation of the fines? I would still keep the militia as an organized body of men, and should there be a real necessity to call them forth, pay them out of the proper revenues of the state, and increase the taxes a third or fourth per cent., on those who do not attend.

My limits will not allow me to go further into this matter, which I shall therefore close with this remark; that fines are, of all modes of revenue, the most unsuited to the mind of a free country. When a man pays a tax, he knows that the public necessity requires it, and therefore feels a pride in discharging his duty; but a fine seems an atonement for neglect of duty, and of consequence is paid with discredit, and frequently levied with severity.

I have now only one subject more to speak of, with which I shall conclude, which is, the resolve of Congress of the 18th of March last, for taking up and funding the present currency at forty for one, and issuing new money in its stead.

Every one knows that I am not a flatterer of Congress, but in this instance *they are right*; and if that measure is supported, the currency will acquire a value, which, without it, it will not. But this is not all: it will give relief to the finances until, such time as they can be properly arranged, and save the country from being immediately double taxed under the present mode. In short, support that measure, and it will support you.

I have now waded through a tedious cause of difficult business, and over an untrodden path. The subject, on every point in which it could be viewed, was entangled with perplexities, and enveloped in obscurity, yet such are the resources of America, that she wants nothing but system to secure success.

COMMON SENSE.
Philadelphia, Oct. 6, 1780.

THE CRISIS
NUMBER XI

On the King of England's Speech

O F all the innocent passions which actuate the human mind, there is none more universally prevalent than curiosity. It reaches all mankind, and in matters which concern us, or concern us not, it alike provokes in us a desire to know them.

Although the situation of America, superior to every effort to enslave her, and daily rising to importance and opulence, hath placed her above the region of anxiety, it has still left her within the circle of curiosity; and her fancy to see the speech of a man who had proudly threatened to bring her to his feet, was visibly marked with that tranquil confidence which cared nothing about its contents. It was inquired after with a smile, read with a laugh, and dismissed with disdain.

But, as justice is due, even to an enemy, it is right to say, that the speech is as well managed as the embarrassed condition of their affairs could well admit of; and though hardly a line of it is true, except the mournful story of Cornwallis, it may serve to amuse the deluded commons and people of England, for whom it was calculated.

"The war," says the speech, "is still unhappily prolonged by that restless ambition which first excited our enemies to commence it, and which still continues to disappoint my earnest wishes and diligent exertions to restore the public tranquillity."

How easy it is to abuse truth and language, when men, by habitual wickedness, have learned to set justice at defiance. That the very man who began the war, who with the most sullen insolence refused to answer, and even to hear the humblest of all petitions, who hath encouraged his officers and his army in the most savage cruelties, and the most scandalous plunderings, who hath stirred up the Indians on one side, and the negroes on the other, and invoked every aid of hell in his behalf, should now, with an affected air of pity, turn the tables from himself, and charge to another the wickedness that is his own, can only be equalled by the baseness of the heart that spoke it.

To be nobly wrong is more manly than to be meanly right, is an expression I once used on a former occasion, and it is equally applicable now. We feel something like respect for consistency even in error. We lament the virtue that is debauched into a vice, but the vice that effects a virtue becomes the more detestable: and amongst the various assumptions of character, which hypocrisy has taught, and men have practised, there is none that raises a higher relish of disgust, than to see disappointed inveteracy twisting itself; by the most visible falsehoods, into an appearance of piety it has no pretensions to.

"But I should not," continues the speech, "answer the trust committed to the sovereign of a *free people*, nor make a suitable return to my subjects for their constant, zealous, and affectionate attachment to my person, family and government, if I consented to sacrifice, either to my own desire of peace, or to their temporary ease and relief, *those essential rights and permanent interests*, upon the maintenance and preservation of which the future strength and security of this country must principally depend."

That the man whose ignorance and obstinacy first involved and still continues the nation in the most hopeless and expensive of all wars, should now meanly flatter them with the name of a *free people*, and make a merit of his crime, under the disguise of their essential rights and permanent interests, is something which disgraces even the character of perverseness. Is he afraid they will send him to Hanover, or what does he fear? Why is the sycophant thus added to the hypocrite, and the man who pretends to govern, sunk into the humble and submissive memorialist?

What those essential rights and permanent interests are, on which the future strength and security of England must principally *depend*, are not so much as alluded to. They are words which impress nothing but the ear, and are calculated only for the sound.

But if they have any reference to America, then do they amount to the disgraceful confession, that England, who once assumed to be her protectress, has now become her *dependant*. The British king and ministry are constantly holding up the vast importance which America is of to England, in order to allure the nation to carry on the war: now, whatever ground there is for this idea, it ought to have operated as a reason for not beginning it; and, therefore, they support their present measures at their own disgrace, because the arguments they now use are a direct reflection on their former policy.

"The favorable appearance of affairs," continues the speech, "in the East, Indies, and the safe arrival of the numerous commercial fleets of my kingdom, must have given you satisfaction."

That things are not *quite* so bad every where as in America may be some cause of consolation, but can be none for triumph. One broken leg is better than two, but still it is not a source of joy: and let the appearance of affairs in the East Indies be ever so favorable, they are nevertheless worse than at first, without a prospect of their ever being better. But the mournful story of Cornwallis was yet to be told, and it was necessary to give it the softest introduction possible.

"But in the course of this year," continues the speech, "my assiduous endeavors to guard the extensive dominions of my crown, have not been attended with success equal to the justice and uprightness of my views.—" What justice and uprightness there was in beginning a war with America, the world will judge of, and the unequalled barbarity with which it has been conducted, is not to be worn from the memory by the cant of snivelling hypocrisy.

"And it is with *great concern* that I inform you that the events of war have been very unfortunate to my arms in Virginia, having ended in the loss of my forces in that province."—And *our* great concern is that they are not all served in the same manner.

"No endeavors have been wanting on my part," says the speech, "to extinguish that spirit of rebellion which our enemies have found means to foment and maintain in the colonies; and to restore to my *deluded subjects* in America that happy and prosperous condition which they formerly derived from a due obedience to the laws."

The expression of *deluded subjects* is become so hacknied and contemptible, and the more so when we see them making prisoners of whole armies at a time, that the pride of not being laughed at would induce a man of common sense to leave it off. But the most offensive falsehood in the paragraph, is the attributing the prosperity of America to a wrong cause. It was the unremitted industry of the settlers and their descendants, the hard labor and toil of persevering fortitude, that were the true causes of the prosperity of America. The former tyranny of England served to people it, and the virtue of the adventurers to improve it. Ask the man who with his axe hath cleared a way in the wilderness and now possesses an estate, what made him rich, and he will tell you the labor of his hands, the sweat of his brow, and the blessing of heaven. Let Britain but leave America to herself and she asks no more. She has risen into greatness without the knowledge and against the will of England, and has a right to the unmolested enjoyment of her own created wealth.

"I will order," says the speech, "the estimates of the ensuing year to be laid before you. I rely on your wisdom and public spirit for such supplies as the circumstances of our affairs shall be found to require. Among the many ill consequences which attend the continuation of the present war, I must sincerely regret the additional burdens which it must unavoidably bring upon my faithful subjects."

Strange! That a nation must run through such a labyrinth of trouble, and expend such a mass of wealth to gain the wisdom which an hour's reflection might have taught. The final superiority of America over every attempt which an island might make to conquer her, was as naturally marked in the constitution of things, as the future ability of a giant over a dwarf is delineated in his features while an infant. How far Providence, to accomplish purposes, which no human wisdom could foresee, permitted such extraordinary errors, will be believed by some and doubted by others, is still a secret in the womb of time, and must remain so till futurity shall give it birth.

"In the prosecution of this great and important contest," says the speech, "in which we are engaged, I retain a firm confidence in the *protection of divine Providence,* and a perfect conviction in the justice of my cause, and I have no doubt, but that, by the concurrence and support of my parliament, by the valor of my fleets and armies, and by a vigorous, animated, and united exertion of the faculties and resources of my people, I shall be enabled to restore the blessings of a safe and honorable peace to all my dominions."

The king of England is one of the readiest believers in the world. In the beginning of the contest he passed an act to put America out of the protection of the crown of England, and though Providence, for seven years together hath put him out of *her* protection, still the man has no doubt. Like Pharoah on the edge of the Red Sea, he sees not the plunge he is making, and precipitately drives across the flood that is closing over his head.

I think it is a reasonable supposition, that this part of the speech was composed before the arrival of the news of the capture of Cornwallis: for it certainly has no relation to their condition at the time it was spoken. But, be this as it may, it is nothing to us. Our line is fixed. Our lot is cast. And America, the child of fate, is arriving at maturity. We have nothing to do but by a spirited and quick exertion, to stand prepared for war or peace. Too great to yield, and too noble to insult; superior to misfortune, and generous in success, let us untaintedly preserve the character we have gained, and show to future ages, an example of unequalled magnanimity.

There is something in the cause and consequence of America that has drawn on her the attention of all mankind. The world has seen her brave. Her love of liberty; her ardor in supporting it; the justice of her claims, and the constancy of her fortitude has won her the esteem of Europe, and attached to her interest the first power of that country.

Her situation now is such, that to whatever point, past, present or to come she casts her eyes, new matter arises to convince her she is right. In her conduct towards her enemy, no reproachful sentiment lurks in secret. No sense of injustice is left upon the mind.

Untainted with ambition and a stranger to revenge, her progress hath been marked by Providence, and she, in every stage of the conflict, hath blessed her with success.

But let not America wrap herself up in delusive hope and suppose the business done. The least remissness in preparation, the least relaxation in execution, will only serve to prolong the war and increase expenses. If our enemies can draw consolation from misfortune and exert themselves upon despair, how much more ought we, who are to win a continent by the conquest and have already an earnest of success?

Having in the preceding part made my remarks on the several matters which the speech contains, I shall now make my remarks on what it does not contain.

There is not a syllable in it respecting alliances. Either the injustice of Britain is too glaring, or her condition too desperate, or both, for any neighboring power to come to her support. In the beginning of the contest, when she had only America to contend with, she hired assistance from Hesse and other smaller states of Germany, and for nearly three years did America, young, raw, undisciplined and unprovided, stand against the power of Britain, aided by twenty thousand foreign troops, and made a complete conquest of one entire army. The remembrance of those things ought to inspire us with confidence and greatness of mind, and carry us through every remaining difficulty with content and cheerfulness. What are the little sufferings of the present day, compared with the hardships that are past. There was a time, when we had neither house nor home in safety; when every hour was the hour of alarm and danger; when the mind, tortured with anxiety knew no repose, and every thing but hope and fortitude, was bidding us farewell.

It is of use to look back upon these things; to call to mind the times of trouble and the scenes of complicated anguish that are past and, gone. Then every expense was cheap, compared with the dread of conquest and the misery of submission. We did not stand debating upon trifles, nor contending about the necessary and unavoidable charges of defence. Every one bore his lot of suffering, and looked forward to happier days and scenes of rest.

Perhaps one of the greatest dangers which any country can be exposed to, arises from a kind of trifling which sometimes steals upon the mind, when it supposes the danger past; and this unsafe situation marks at this time the peculiar crisis of America. What would she once have given to have known that her condition at this day should be what it now is? And yet we do not seem to place a proper value upon it, nor vigorously pursue the necessary measures to secure it. We know that we cannot be defended, nor yet defend ourselves, without trouble and expense. We have no right to expect it; neither ought we to look for it. We are a people, who, in our situation, differ from all the world. We form one common floor of public good, and, whatever is our charge, it is paid for our own interest and upon our own account.

Misfortune and experience have now taught us system and method; and the arrangements for carrying on the war are reduced to rule and order. The quota of the several states are ascertained, and I intend in a future publication to show what they are, and the necessity as well as the advantages of vigorously providing them.

In the mean time, I shall conclude this paper with an

instance of *British clemency*, from Smollett' s *History of England*, vol. xi, page 239, printed in London. It will serve to show how dismal is the situation of a conquered people, and that the only security is an effectual defence.

We all know that the Stuart family and the house of Hanover opposed each other for the crown of England. The Stuart family stood first in the line of succession, but the other was the most successful.

In July, 1745, Charles, the son of the exiled king, landed in Scotland, collected a small force, at no time exceeding five or six thousand men, and made some attempts to re-establish his claim. The late Duke of Cumberland, uncle to the present king of England, was sent against him, and on the 16th of April following, Charles was totally defeated at Culloden, in Scotland. Success and power are the only situations in which clemency can be shown, and those who are cruel, because they are victorious, can with the same facility act any other degenerate character.

"Immediately after the decisive action at Culloden, the Duke of Cumberland took possession of Inverness; where six and thirty deserters, convicted by a court martial, were ordered to be executed: then he detached several parties to ravage the country. One of these apprehended the lady Mackintosh, (who was sent prisoner to Inverness,) plundered her house, and drove away her cattle, though her husband was actually in the service of the government. The castle of Lord Lovat was destroyed. The French prisoners were sent to Carlisle and Penrith. Kilmarnock, Balmerino, Cromartie and his son, the Lord Macleod, were conveyed by sea to London; and those of an inferior rank were confined in different prisons. The Marquis of Tullibardine, together with a brother of the Earl of Dunmore, and Murray, the pretender's secretary, were seized and

transported to the tower of London, to which the Earl of
Traquaire had been committed on suspicion; and the eldest son
of Lord Lovat was imprisoned in the castle of Edinburgh. In a
word, all the jails in Great Britain, from the capital, north-
wards, were filled with those unfortunate captives; and great
numbers of them were crowded together in the holds of ships,
where they perished in the most deplorable manner, for want
of air and exercise. Some rebel chiefs escaped in two French
frigates that arrived on the coast of Lochaber about the end of
April, and engaged three vessels belonging to his Britannic
majesty, which they obliged to retire. Others embarked on
board a ship on the coast of Buchan, and were conveyed to
Norway, from whence they travelled to Sweden. In the month
of May, the Duke of Cumberland advanced with the army into
the Highlands, as far as Fort Augustus, where he encamped;
and sent off detachments on all hands, to hunt down the fugi-
tives, and lay waste the country with fire and sword. The cas-
tles of Glengary and Lochiel were plundered and burned;
every house, hut, or habitation met with the same fate without
distinction, and all the cattle and provision were carried off.
The men were either shot upon the mountains, like wild beasts,
or put to death in cold blood, without form or trial,—the
women, after having seen their husbands and fathers murdered
were subjected to brutal violation, and then turned out naked,
with their children, to starve on the barren heaths. One whole
family was enclosed in a barn, and consumed to ashes. Those
ministers of vengeance were so alert in the execution of their
office, that in a few days there was neither house, cottage, man,
nor beast, to be seen within the compass of fifty miles; all was
ruin, silence, and desolation."

I have here presented the reader with one of the most
shocking instances of cruelty ever practised, and I leave it to

rest on his mind, that he may be fully impressed with a sense of the destruction he has escaped, in case Britain had conquered America; and likewise, that he may see and feel the necessity, as well for his own personal safety, as for the honor, the interest, and happiness of the whole community, to omit or delay no one preparation necessary to secure the ground which we so happily stand upon.

To the People of America
ON THE EXPENSES, ARRANGEMENTS AND DISBURSEMENTS
FOR CARRYING ON THE WAR, AND FINISHING IT WITH
HONOR AND ADVANTAGE.

WHEN any necessity or occasion has pointed out the convenience of addressing the public, I have never made it a consideration whether the subject was popular or unpopular, but whether it was right or wrong; for that which is right will become popular, and that which is wrong, though by mistake it may obtain the cry or fashion of the day, will soon lose the power of delusion, and sink into disesteem.

A remarkable instance of this happened in the case of Silas Deane; and I mention this circumstance with the greater ease, because the poison of his hypocrisy spread over the whole country, and every man, almost without exception, thought me wrong in opposing him. The best friends I then had, except Mr. Laurens, stood at a distance, and this tribute, which is due to his constancy, I pay to him with respect, and that the readier, because he is not here to hear it. If it reaches him in his imprisonment, it will afford him an agreeable reflection.

"*As he rose like a rocket, he will fall like the stick,*" is a metaphor which I applied to Mr. Deane in the first piece which I published respecting him, and he has exactly fulfilled the description. The credit he so unjustly obtained from the public, he lost in almost as short a time. The delusion perished as it fell, and he soon saw himself stripped of popular support. His more intimate acquaintances began to doubt and to desert him long before he left America, and at his departure he saw himself the object of general suspicion. When he arrived in France, he endeavored to effect by treason what he had failed to accomplish by fraud. His plans, schemes and projects, together with his expectation of being sent to Holland to negotiate a loan of money, had all miscarried. He then began traducing and accusing America of every crime, which could injure her reputation. "That she was a ruined country; that she only meant to make a tool of France, to get what money she could out of her, and then to leave her, and accommodate with Britain." Of all which, and much more, Colonel Laurens and myself, when in France, informed Dr. Franklin, who had not before heard of it. And to complete the character of a traitor, he has, by letters to this country since, (some of which in his own hand writing are now in the possession of Congress,) used every expression and argument in his power to injure the reputation of France, and to advise America to renounce her alliance, and surrender up her independence.* Thus in France, he abuses America, and in his letters to America he abuses France; and is endeavoring to create disunion between the two countries, by the same arts of double-dealing by which he caused dissensions among the commissioners in Paris, and distractions in America. But his life has been fraud, and his character is that of a plodding, plot-

---

* Mr. William Marshall, of this city, formerly a pilot, who had been taken at sea and carried to England, and got from thence to France, brought over letters from Mr. Deane to America, one of which was directed to "Robert Morris, Esq." Mr. Morris sent it unopened to Congress and advised Mr. Marshall to deliver the others there, which he did. The letters were of the same purport with those which have been already published under the signature of S. Deane, to which they had frequent reference.

ting, cringing mercenary, capable of any disguise that suited his purpose. His final detection has very happily cleared up those mistakes, and removed that uneasiness, which his unprincipled conduct occasioned. Every one now sees him in the same light; for towards friends or enemies he acted with the same deception and injustice, and his name, like that of *Arnold*, ought now to be forgotten among us. As this is the first time I have mentioned him since my return from France, it is my intention it shall be the last. From this digression, which for several reasons I thought necessary to give, I now proceed to the purport of my address.

I consider the war of America against Britain as the country's war, the public's war, or the war of the people in their own behalf, for the security of their natural rights and the protection of their own property. It is not the war of Congress, the war of the Assemblies, or the war of government, in any line whatever. The country first, by a mutual compact, resolved to defend their rights and maintain their independence, *at the hazard of their lives and fortunes.* They elected their representatives by whom they appointed their members to Congress, and said, *act you for us, and we will support you.* This is the true ground and principle of the war on the part of America, and consequently, there remains nothing to do, but for every one to fulfill his obligation.

It was next to impossible that a new country, engaged in a new undertaking, could set off systematically right at first. She saw not the extent of the struggle she was involved in, neither could she avoid the beginning. She supposed every step she took, and every resolution she formed, would bring her enemy to reason, and close the contest. Those failing, she was forced into new measures; and these, like the former, being fitted to her expectations, and failing in their turn, left her continually unprovided and without system. The enemy likewise was induced to prosecute the war, from the temporary expedients we adopted for carrying it on. We were continually expecting to see their credit exhausted, and they were looking to see our currency fail; and thus, between their watching us and we them, the hopes of both have been deceived, and the childishness of the expectation has served to increase the expense.

Yet who, through this wilderness of error, has been to blame? Where if the man who can say, the fault has not in part been his? They were the natural, unavoidable errors of the day. They were the errors of a whole country, which nothing but experience could detect, and time remove. Neither could the circumstances of America admit of system, till either the paper currency was fixed or laid aside. No calculation of finance could be made on a medium failing without reason, and fluctuating without rule.

But there is one error which might have been prevented, and was not; and as it is not my custom to flatter, but to serve mankind, I will speak it freely. It certainly was the duty of every assembly on the continent to have known, at all times, what was the condition of its treasury, and to have ascertained at every period of deprcciation, how much the real worth of the taxes fell short of their nominal value. This knowledge, which might have been easily obtained, would have enabled them to have kept their constituents well informed, which is one of the greatest duties of representation. They ought to have studied and calculated the expenses of the war, the quota of each state, and the consequent proportion that would fall on each man's property for his defence; and this must easily have shown to them, that a tax of one hundred pounds could not be paid by a bushel of apples or an hundred of flour, which was often the case two or three years ago. But instead of this, which would have been plain and upright dealing, the little line of temporary popularity, the feather of an hour's duration, was too much pursued; and in this involved condition of things, every state, for the want of a little thinking, or a little information, supposed that it supported the whole expenses of the war, when in fact it fell, by the time the tax was levied and collected, above three-fourths short of its own quota.

Impressed with a sense of the danger to which the country was exposed by this lax method of doing business, and the prevailing errors of the day, I published, last October was a twelvemonth, *The Crisis Extraordinary*, on the revenues of America, and the yearly expense of carrying on the war. My estimation of the latter, together with the civil list of Congress, and the civil list of the several states, was two million pounds sterling, which is very nearly nine millions of dollars.

Since that time, Congress have gone into a calculation, and have estimated the expenses of the war department and the civil list of Congress (exclusive of the civil list of the several governments) at eight millions of dollars; and as the remaining million will be fully sufficient for the civil list of the several states, the two calculations are exceedingly near each other.

The sum of eight millions of dollars they have called upon the states to furnish, and their quotas are as follows, which I shall preface with the resolution itself.

"BY THE UNITED STATES IN CONGRESS ASSEMBLED. *October 30, 1781.*

"*Resolved,* That the respective states be called upon to furnish the Treasury of the United States with their quotas of eight millions of dollars, for the war department and civil list for the ensuing year, to be paid quarterly, in equal proportions, the first payment to be made on the first day of April next.

"*Resolved*, That a committee consisting of a member from each state, be appointed to apportion to the several states the quota of the above sum.

"*November 2nd*. The committee appointed to ascertain the proportions of the several states of the monies to be raised for the expenses of the ensuing year, report the following resolutions:

"That the sum of eight millions of dollars, as required to be raised by the resolutions of the 30th of October last, be paid by the states in the following proportion:

New Hampshire	$373,598
Massachusetts	1,307,596
Rhode Island	216,684
Connecticut	747,196
New York	373,598
New Jersey	485,679
Pennsylvania	1,120,794
Delaware	112,085
Maryland	933,996
Virginia	1,307,594
North Carolina	622,677
South Carolina	373,598
Georgia	24,905
	$8,000,000

"*Resolved*, That it be recommended to the several states, to lay taxes for raising their quotas of money for the United States, separate from those laid for their own particular use."

On these resolutions I shall offer several remarks.

First, On the sum itself, and the ability of the country.

Secondly, On the several quotas, and the nature of a union. And,

Thirdly, On the manner of collection and expenditure.

First, On the sum itself, and the ability of the country. As I know my own calculation is as low as possible, and as the sum called for by Congress, according to their calculation, agrees very nearly therewith, I am sensible it cannot possibly be lower. Neither can it be done for that, unless there is ready money to go to market with; and even in that case, it is only by the utmost management and economy that it can be made to do.

By the accounts which were laid before the British parliament last spring, it appeared that the charge of only subsisting, that is, feeding their army in America, cost annually four million pounds sterling, which is very nearly eighteen millions of dollars. Now if, for eight millions, we can feed, clothe, arm, provide for and pay an army sufficient for our defence, the very comparison shows that the money must be well laid out.

It may be of some use, either in debate or conversation, to attend to the progress of the expenses of an army, because it will enable us to see on what part any deficiency will fall. The *first* thig is, to feed them and provide for the sick. *Secondly*, to clothe them. *Thirdly*, to arm and furnish them. *Fourthly*, to provide means for removing them from place to place. And, *Fifthly*, to pay them.

The first and second are absolutely necessary to them as men. The third and fourth are equally as necessary to them as an army. And the fifth is their just due. Now, if the sum which shall be raised should fall short, either by the several acts of the states for raising it, or by the manner of collecting it, the deficiency will fall on the fifth head, the soldier's pay, which would be defrauding them, and eternally disgracing ourselves.

It would be a blot on the councils, the country, and the revolution of America, and a man would hereafter be ashamed to own he had any hand in it.

But if the deficiency should be still shorter, it would next fall on the fourth head, *the means of moving the army from place to place*: and in this case, the army must either stand still where it can be of no use, or seize on horses, carts, wagons, or any means of transportation which it can lay hold of; and in this instance the country suffers. In short, every attempt to do a thing for less than it can be done for, is sure to become at last both a loss and a dishonor.

But the country cannot bear it, say some. This has been the most expensive doctrine that ever was held out, and cost America millions of money for nothing. Can the country bear to be overrun, ravaged, and ruined by an enemy? This will immediately follow where defence is wanting, and defence will ever be wanting where sufficient revenues are not provided. But this is only one part of the folly. The second is, that when the danger comes, invited in part by our not preparing against it, we have been obliged, in a number of instances, to expend double the sums to do that which at first might have been done for half the money. But this is not all. A third mischief has been, that grain of all sorts, flour, beef, fodder, horses, carts, wagons, or whatever was absolutely or immediately wanted, have been taken without pay. Now, I ask, why was all this done, but from that extremely weak and expensive doctrine, *that the country could not bear it*? That is, that she could not bear, in the first instance, that which would have saved her twice as much at last; or, in proverbial language, that she could not bear to pay a penny to save a pound; the consequence of which has been, that she has paid a pound for a penny. Why are there so many unpaid certificates in almost every man's hands, but from the parsimony of not providing sufficient revenues? Besides, the doctrine contradicts itself; because, if the whole country cannot bear it, how is it possible that a part should? And yet this has been the case; for those things have been had; and they must be had; but the misfortune is, that they have been obtained in a very unequal manner, and upon expensive credit, whereas, with ready money, they might have been purchased for half the price, and nobody distressed.

But there is another thought which ought to strike us, which is: How is the army to bear the want of food, clothing and other necessaries? The man who is at home, can turn himself a thousand ways, and find as many means of ease, convenience or relief; but a soldier's life admits of none of these; their wants cannot be supplied from themselves; for an army, though it is the defence of a state, is at the same time the child of a country, and must be provided for in every thing.

And lastly, The doctrine is false. There are not three millions of people in any part of the universe, who live so well, or have such a fund of ability as in America. The income of a common laborer, who is industrious, is equal to that of the generality of tradesmen in England.

In the mercantile line, I have not heard of one who could be said to be a bankrupt since the war began, and in England they have been without number. In America almost every farmer lives on his own lands, and in England not one in a hundred does. In short, it seems as if the poverty of that country had made them furious, and they were determined to risk all to recover all.

Yet, notwithstanding those advantages on the part of America, true it is, that had it not been for the operation of taxes for our necessary defence, we had sunk into a state of sloth and poverty: for there was more wealth lost by neglecting to till the earth in the years 1776, '77, and '78, than the quota of the tax amounts to. That which is lost by neglect of this kind, is lost for ever: whereas that which is paid, and continues in the country, returns to us again; and at the same time that it provides us with defence, it operates not only as a spur, but as a premium to our industry.

I shall now proceed to the second head, *viz., on the several quotas, and the nature of a union.*

There was a time when America had no other bond of union, than that of common interest and affection. The whole country flew to the relief of Boston, and making her cause their own, participated in her cares and administered to her wants. The fate of war, since that day, has carried the calamity in a ten-fold proportion to the southward; but in the mean time the union has been strengthened by a legal compact of the states, jointly and severally ratified, and that which before was choice, or the duty of affection, is now likewise the duty of legal obligation.

The union of America is the foundation-stone of her independence—the rock on which it is built; and is something so sacred in her constitution, that we ought to watch every word we speak, and every thought we think, that we injure it not, even by mistake. When a multitude, extended, or rather scattered over a continent in the manner we are, mutually agree to form one common centre whereon the whole shall move to accomplish a particular purpose, all parts must act together and alike, or act not at all, and a stoppage in any one is a stoppage of the whole, at least for a time.

Thus the several states have sent representatives to assemble together in Congress, and they have empowered that body, which thus becomes their centre, and are no other than themselves in representation, to conduct and manage the war, while their constituents at home attend to the domestic cares of the country, their internal legislation, their farms, professions or employments. For it is only reducing complicated things to method and orderly connection that they can be understood with advantage, or pursued with success. Congress, by virtue of this delegation, estimates the expense, and apportions it out to the several parts of the empire according to their several abilities; and here the debate must end, because each state has already had its voice, and the matter has undergone its whole portion of argument, and can no more be altered by any particular state, than a law of any state, after it has passed, can be altered by any individual. For with respect to those things which immediately concern the union, and for which the union was purposely established, and is intended to secure, each state is to the United States what each individual is to the state he lives in. And it is on this grand point, this movement upon one centre, that our existence as a nation, our happiness as a people, and our safety as individuals depend.

It may happen that some state or other may be somewhat over or under rated, but this cannot be much. The experience which has been had upon the matter, has nearly ascertained their several abilities. But even in this case, it can only admit of an appeal to the United States, but cannot authorize any state to make the alteration itself, any more than our internal government can admit an individual to do so in the case of an act of assembly; for if one state can do it, then may another do the same, and the instant this is done the whole is undone.

Neither is it supposable that any single state can be a judge of all the comparative reasons which may influence the collective body in arranging the quotas of the continent. The circumstances of the several states are frequently varying, occasioned by the accidents of war and commerce, and it will often fall upon some to help others, rather beyond what their exact proportion at another time might be; but even this assistance is as naturally and politically included in the idea of a union, as that of any particular assigned proportion; because we know not whose turn it may be next to want assistance, for which reason that is the wisest state which sets the best example.

Though in matters of bounden duty and reciprocal affection, it is rather a degeneracy from the honesty and ardor of the heart to admit any thing selfish to partake in the government of our conduct, yet in cases where our duty, our affections, and our interest all coincide, it may be of some use to observe their union. The United States will become heir to an extensive quantity of vacant land, and their several titles to shares and quotas thereof, will naturally be adjusted according to their relative quotas, during the war, exclusive of that inability which may unfortunately arise to any state by the enemy holding possession of a part; but as this is a cold matter of interest, I pass it by, and proceed to my third head, *viz.*

On the Manner of Collection and Expenditure

It hath been our error, as well as our misfortune, to blend the affairs of each state, especially in money matters, with those of the United States; whereas it is to our ease, convenience and interest to keep them separate. The expenses of the United States for carrying on the war, and the expenses of each state for its own domestic government, are distinct things, and to involve them is a source of perplexity and a cloak for fraud. I love method, because I see and am convinced of its beauty and advantage. It is that which makes all business easy and understood, and without which every thing becomes embarassed and difficult.

There are certain powers which the people of each state have delegated to their legislative and executive bodies, and there are other powers which the people of every state have delegated to Congress, among which is that of conducting the war, and consequently, of managing the expenses attending it; for how else can that be managed, which concerns every state, but by a delegation from each? When a state has furnished its quota, it has an undoubted right to know how it has been applied, and it is as much the duty of Congress to inform the state of the one, as it is the duty of the state to provide the other.

In the resolution of Congress already recited, it is recommended to the several states *to lay faxes for raising their quotas of money for the United States, separate from those laid for their own particular use.*

This is a most necessary point to be observed, and the distinction should follow all the way through. They should be levied, paid and collected separately, and kept separate in every instance. Neither have the civil officers of any state, or the government of that state, the least right to touch that money which the people pay for the support of their army and the war, any more than Congress has to touch that which each state raises for its own use.

This distinction will naturally be followed by another. It will occasion every state to examine nicely into the expenses of its civil list, and to regulate, reduce and bring it into better order than it has hitherto been; because the money for that purpose must be raised apart, and accounted for to the public separately. But while the moneys of both were blended, the necessary nicety was not observed, and the poor soldier, who ought to have been the first, was the last who was thought of.

Another convenience will be, that the people, by paying

the taxes separately, will know what they are for; and will likewise know that those which are for the defence of the country will cease with the war, or soon after. For although, as I have before observed, the war is their own, and for the support of their own rights and the protection of their own property, yet they have the same right to know, that they have to pay, and it is the want of not knowing that is often the cause of dissatisfaction. This regulation of keeping the taxes separate has given rise to a regulation in the office of finance, by which it is directed.

"That the receivers shall, at the end of every month, make out an exact account of the monies received by them respectively, during such month, specifying therein the names of the persons from whom the same shall have been received, the dates and the sums; which account they shall respectively cause to be published in one of the newspapers of the state; to the end that every citizen may know how much of the monies collected from him in taxes, is transmitted to the treasury of the United States for the support of the war; and also, that it may be known what monies have been at the order of the superintendent of finance. It being proper and necessary that, in a free country, the people should be as fully informed of the administration of their affairs as the nature of things will admit."

It is an agreeable thing to see a spirit of order and economy taking place, after such a series of errors and difficulties. A government or an administration, that means and acts honestly, has nothing to fear, and consequently has nothing to conceal; and it would be of use if a monthly or quarterly account was to be published, as well of the expenditures as of the receipts. Eight millions of dollars must be husbanded with an exceeding deal of care to make it do, and therefore, as the management must be reputable, the publication would be serviceable.

I have heard of petitions which have been presented to the assembly of this state (and probably the same may have happened in other states) praying to have the taxes lowered. Now the only way to keep taxes low, is for the United States to have ready money to go to market with; and though the taxes to be raised for the present year will fall heavy, and there will naturally be some difficulty in paying them, yet the difficulty, in proportion as money spreads about the country, will every day grow less, and in the end we shall save some millions of dollars by it. We see what a bitter, revengeful enemy we have to deal with, and any expense is cheap compared to their merciless paw. We have seen the unfortunate Carolineans hunted like partridges on the mountains, and it is only by providing means for our defence, that we shall be kept from the same condition. When we think or talk about taxes, we ought to recollect that we lie down in peace and sleep in safety—that we can follow our farms or stores or other occupations, in prosperous tranquillity; and that these inestimable blessings are procured to us by the taxes that we pay. In this view, our taxes are properly our insurance money; they are what we pay to be made safe, and in strict policy are the best money we can lay out.

It was my intention to offer some remarks on the impost law of five per cent. recommended by Congress, and to be established as a fund for the payment of the loan-office certificates, and other debts of the United States; but I have already extended my piece beyond my intention. And as this fund will make our system of finance complete, and is strictly just, and consequently requires nothing but honesty to do it, there needs but little to be said upon it.

COMMON SENSE.
Philadelphia, March 5, 1782.

THE CRISIS
NUMBER XII

On the Present State of News

SINCE the arrival of two, if not three packets, in quick succession, at New York, from England, a variety of unconnected *news* has circulated through the country, and afforded as great a variety of speculation.

That something is the matter in the cabinet and councils of our enemies, on the other side of the water, is certain—that they have run their length of madness and are under the necessity of changing their measures, may easily be seen into; but to what this change of measures may amount, or how far it may correspond with our interest, happiness and duty, is yet uncertain; and from what we have hitherto experienced, we have too much reason to suspect them in every thing.

I do not address this publication so much to the people of America as to the British ministry, whoever they may be, for if it is their intention to promote any kind of negotiation, it is proper they should know beforehand, that the United States have as much honor as bravery; and that they are no more to be seduced from their alliance than their allegiance; that their line of politics is formed and not dependant; like that of their enemy, on chance and accident.

On our part, in order to know, at any time, what the British government will do, we have only to find out what they ought *not* to do, and this last will be their conduct. Forever changing and forever wrong; too distant from America to improve circumstances, and too unwise to foresee them; scheming without principle, and executing without probability, their whole line of management has hitherto been blunder and baseness. Every campaign has added to their loss, and every year to their disgrace: till unable to go on, and ashamed to go back, their politics have come to a halt, and all their fine prospects to a halter.

Could our affections forgive, or humanity forget the wounds of an injured country—we might, under the influence of a momentary oblivion, stand still and laugh. But they are engraven where no amusement can conceal them, and of a kind for which there is no recompense. Can ye restore to us the beloved dead? Can ye say to the grave, give up the murdered? Can ye obliterate from our memories those who are no more? Think not then to tamper with our feelings by insidious contrivance, nor suffocate our humanity by seducing us to dishonor.

In March, 1780, I published part of the *Crisis*, No. VIII, in the newspapers, but did not conclude it in the following papers, and the remainder has lain by me till the present day.

There appeared about that time some disposition in the British cabinet to cease the further prosecution of the war, and as I had formed my opinion that whenever such a design should take place, it would be accompanied with a dishonorable proposition to America, respecting France, I had suppressed the remainder of that number, not to expose the baseness of any such proposition. But the arrival of the next news from England, declared her determination to go on with the war, and consequently as the political object I had then in view was not really a subject, it was unnecessary in me to bring it forward, which is the reason it was never published.

The matter which I allude to in the unpublished part, I shall now make a quotation of, and apply it as the more enlarged state of things, at this day, shall make convenient or necessary.

It was as follows:

"By the speeches which have appeared from the British parliament, it is easy to perceive to what impolitic and imprudent excesses their passions and prejudices have, in every instance, carried them during the present war. Provoked at the upright and honorable treaty between America and France, they imagined that nothing more was necessary to be done to prevent its final ratification, than to promise, through the agency of their commissioners (Carlisle, Eden, and Johnston) a repeal of their once offensive acts of parliament. The vanity of the conceit was as unpardonable as the experiment was impolitic. And so convinced am I of their wrong ideas of America, that I shall not wonder, if in their last stage of political frenzy, they propose to her to break her alliance with France, and enter into one with them. Such a proposition, should it ever be made, and it has already been more than once hinted at in parliament, would discover such a disposition to perfidiousness and such disregard of honor and morals, as would add the finishing vice to national corruption. I do not mention this to put America on the watch, but to put England on her guard, that she do not, in the looseness of her heart, envelope in disgrace every fragment of reputation." Thus far the quotation.

By the complexion of some part of the news which has transpired through the New York papers, it seems probable that this insidious era in the British politics is beginning to make its appearance. I wish it may not; for that which is a disgrace to human nature, throws something of a shade over all the human character, and each individual feels his share of the wound that is given to the whole.

The policy of Britain has ever been to divide America in some way or other. In the beginning of the dispute, she practised every art to prevent or destroy the union of the states, well knowing that could she once get them to stand singly, she could conquer them unconditionally. Failing in this project in America, she renewed it in Europe; and after the alliance had taken place, she made secret offers to France to induce her to give up America; and what is still more extraordinary, she at the same time made propositions to Dr. Franklin, then in Paris, the very court to which she was secretly applying, to draw off America from France. But this is not all.

On the 14th of September, 1778, the British court, through their secretary, Lord Weymouth, made application to the Marquis d' Almadovar, the Spanish ambassador at London, to "ask the mediation," for these were the words of the court of Spain, for the purpose of negotiating a peace with France, leaving America (as I shall hereafter show) out of the question. Spain readily offered her mediation, and likewise the city of Madrid as the place of conference, but withal, proposed, that the United States of America should be invited to the treaty, and considered as independent during the time the business was negotiating. But this was not the view of England. She wanted to draw France from the war, that she might uninterruptedly pour out all her force and fury upon America; and being disappointed in this plan, as well through the open and generous conduct of Spain, as the determination of France, she refused the mediation which she had solicited.

I shall now give some extracts from the justifying memorial of the Spanish court, in which she has set the conduct and character of Britain, with respect to America, in a clear and striking point of light.

The memorial, speaking of the refusal of the British court to meet in conference, with commissioners from the United States, who were to be considered as independent during the time of the conference, says:

"It is a thing very extraordinary and even ridiculous, that the court of London, who treats the colonies as independent, not only in acting, but of right, during the war, should have a repugnance to treat them as such only in acting during truce, or suspension of hostilities. The convention of Saratoga; the reputing General Burgoyne as a lawful prisoner, in order to suspend his trial; the exchange and liberation of other prisoners made from the colonies; the having named commissioners to go and supplicate the Americans, at their own doors, request peace of them, and treat with them and the Congress: and, finally, by a thousand other acts of this sort, authorized by the court of London, which have been, and are true signs of the acknowledgment of their independence.

"In aggravation of all the foregoing, at the same time the British cabinet answered the king of Spain in the terms already mentioned, they were insinuating themselves at the court of France by means of secret emissaries, and making very great offers to her to abandon the colonies and make peace with England. But there is yet more; for at this same time the English ministry were treating, by means of another certain emissary, with Dr. Franklin, minister plenipotentiary from the colonies, residing at Paris, to whom they made various proposals to disunite them from France, and accommodate matters with England.

"From what has been observed, it evidently follows, that the whole of the British politics was, to disunite the two courts of Paris and Madrid, by means of the suggestions and offers she separately made to them; and also to, separate the colonies from their treaties and engagements entered into with France, and induce them to arm against the house of Bourbon, or more *probably to oppress them when they found, from breaking their engagements, that they stood alone and without protection.*

"This, therefore, is the net they laid for the American states; that is to say, to tempt them with flattering and very magnificent promises to come to an accommodation with them, exclusive of any intervention of Spain or France, that the British ministry might always remain the arbiters of the fate of the colonies.

"But the Catholic king (the king of Spain) faithful on the one part of the engagements which bind him to the most Christian king (the king of France) his nephew; just and upright on the other to his own subjects, whom he ought to protect and guard against so many insults; and finally, full of humanity and compassion for the Americans and other individuals who suffer in the present war; he is determined to pursue and prosecute it, and to make all the efforts in his power, until he can obtain a solid and permanent peace, with full and satisfactory securities that it shall be observed."

Thus far the memorial, a translation of which into English, may be seen in full, under the head of State Papers, in the Annual Register for 1779, page 367.

The extracts I have here given, serve to show the various endeavors and contrivances of the enemy to draw France from her connection with America, and to prevail on her to make a separate peace with England, leaving America totally out of the question, and at the mercy of a merciless, unprincipled enemy. The opinion, likewise, which Spain has formed of the British cabinet character, for meanness and perfidiousness, is so exactly the opinion of America respecting it, that the memorial, in this instance, contains our own sentiments and language; for people, however remote, who think alike will unavoidably speak alike.

Thus we see the insidious use which Britain endeavored to make of the propositions for peace under the mediation of Spain. I shall now proceed to the second proposition under the mediation of the emperor of Germany and the empress of Russia; the general outline of which was, that a congress of the several powers at war should meet at Vienna, in 1781, to settle preliminaries of peace.

I could wish myself at liberty to make use of all the information I am possessed of on this subject, but as there is a delicacy in the matter, I do not conceive it prudent, at least at present, to make references and quotations in the same manner as I have done with respect to the mediation of Spain, who published the whole proceedings herself; and therefore, what comes from me, on this part of the business, must rest on my own credit with the public, assuring them, that when the whole proceedings, relative to the proposed congress at Vienna, shall appear, they shall find my account not only true but studiously moderate.

We know that at the time this mediation was on the carpet, the expectations of the British king and ministry ran high with respect to the conquest of America. The English packet which was taken with the mail on board, and carried into l' Orient in France, contained letters from Lord G. Germaine to Sir Henry Clinton, which expressed in the fullest terms the ministerial idea of a total conquest. Copies of those letters were sent to Congress and published in the newspapers of last year. Colonel Laurens brought over the originals, some of which, signed in the handwriting of the then secretary, Germaine, are now in my possession.

Filled with these high ideas, nothing could be more insolent towards America than the language of the British court on the proposed mediation. A peace with France and Spain she anxiously solicited; but America, as before, was to be left to her mercy, neither would she hear any proposition for admitting an agent from the United States into the Congress of Vienna.

On the other hand, France, with an open, noble and manly

determination, and the fidelity of a good ally, would hear no proposition for a separate peace, nor even meet in Congress at Vienna, without an agent from America: and likewise, that the independent character of the United States, represented by the agent, should be fully and unequivocally defined and settled before any conference should be entered on. The reasoning of the court of France on the several propositions of the two Imperial courts, which relate to us, is rather in the style of an American than an ally, and she advocated the cause of America as if she had been America herself.—Thus the second mediation, like the first, proved ineffectual.

But since that time a reverse of fortune has overtaken the British arms, and all their high expectations are dashed to the ground. The noble exertions to the southward under General Greene; the successful operations of the allied arms in the Chesapeake; the loss of most of their islands in the West Indies and of Minorca in the Mediterranean; the persevering spirit of Spain against Gibraltar; the expected capture of Jamaica; the failure of making a separate peace with Holland, and the expense of an hundred millions sterling, by which all these fine losses were obtained, have read them a loud lesson of disgraceful misfortune, and necessity has called on them to change their ground.

In this situation of confusion and despair their present councils have no fixed character. It is now the hurricane months of British politics. Every day seems to have a storm of its own, and they are scudding under the bare poles of hope. Beaten, but not humble; condemned, but not penitent; they act like men trembling at fate and catching at a straw. From this convulsion in the entrails of their politics, it is more than probable that the mountain, groaning in labor, will bring forth a mouse as to its size, and a monster in its make. They will try on America the same insidious arts they tried on France and Spain.

We sometimes experience sensations to which language is not equal. The conception is too bulky to be born alive, and in the torture of thinking we stand dumb. Our feelings, imprisoned by their magnitude, find no way out—and, in the struggle of expression every finger tries to be a tongue. The machinery of the body seems too little for the mind, and we look about for helps to show our thoughts by. Such must be the sensation of America, whenever Britain, teeming with corruption, shall propose to her to sacrifice her faith.

But, exclusive of the wickedness, there is a personal offence contained in every such attempt. It is calling us villains; for no man asks another to act the villain unless he believes him inclined to be one. No man attempts to seduce a truly honest woman. It is the supposed looseness of her mind that starts the thoughts of seduction, and he who offers it calls her a prostitute. Our pride is always hurt by the same propositions which offend our principles; for when we are shocked at the crime we are wounded by the suspicion of our compliance.

Could I convey a thought that might serve to regulate the public mind, I would not make the interest of the alliance the basis of defending it. All the world are moved by interest, and it affords them nothing to boast of. But I would go a step higher, and defend it on the ground of honor and principle. That our public affairs have flourished under the alliance—that it was wisely made and has been nobly executed—that by its assistance we are enabled to preserve our country from conquest and expel those who sought our destruction—that it is our true interest to maintain it unimpaired, and that while we do so no enemy can conquer us,—are matters which experience has taught us, and the common good of ourselves, abstracted from principles of faith and honor, would lead us to maintain the connection.

But over and above the mere letter of the alliance, we have been nobly and generously treated, and have had the same respect and attention paid us, as if we had been an old established country. To oblige and be obliged is fair work among mankind, and we want an opportunity of showing to the world that we are a people sensible of kindness and worthy of confidence.

Character is to us, in our present circumstances, of more importance than interest. We are a young nation, just stepping upon the stage of public life, and the eye of the world is upon us to see how we act. We have an enemy who is watching to destroy our reputation, and who will go any length to gain some evidence against us, that may serve to render our conduct suspected, and our character odious; because, could she accomplish this, wicked as it is, the world would withdraw from us, as from a people not to be trusted, and our task would then become difficult.

There is nothing which sets the character of a nation in a higher or lower light with others, than the faithfully fulfilling, or perfidiously breaking of treaties. They are things not to be tampered with; and should Britain, which seems very probable, propose to seduce America into such an act of baseness, it would merit from her some mark of unusual detestation. It is one of those extraordinary instances in which we ought not to be contented with the bare negative of Congress, because it is an affront on the multitude as well as on the government. It goes on the supposition that the public are not honest men, and that they may be managed by contrivance, though they cannot be conquered by arms. But, let the world and Britain know, that we are neither to be bought nor sold. That our mind is great and fixed; our prospect clear; and that we will support our character as firmly as our independence.

But I will go still further: General Conway, who made the motion in the British parliament, for discontinuing *offensive* war in America, is a gentleman of an amiable character. We have no personal quarrel with him. But he feels not as we feel; he is not in our situation, and that alone, without any other explanation, is enough.

The British parliament suppose they have many friends in America, and that when all chance of conquest is over, they will be able to draw her from her alliance with France. Now, if I have any conception of the human heart, they will fail in this more than in anything they have yet tried.

This part of the business is not a question of policy only, but of honor and honesty; and the proposition will have in it something so visibly low and base that their partisans, if they have any, will be ashamed of it. Men are often hurt by a mean action who are not startled at a wicked one, and this will be such a confession of inability, such a declaration of servile thinking, that the scandal of it will ruin all their hopes.

In short, we have nothing to do but to go on with vigor and determination. The enemy is yet in our country. They hold New York, Charleston and Savannah, and the very being in those places is an offence, and a part of offensive war, and until they can be driven from them, or captured in them, it would be folly in us to listen to an idle tale. I take it for granted that the British ministry are sinking under the impossibility of carrying on the war. Let them then come to a fair and open peace with France, Spain, Holland and America in the manner they ought to do; but until then we can have nothing to say to them.

COMMON SENSE.
Philadelphia, May 22, 1782.

THE CRISIS
NUMBER XIII

To Sir Guy Carleton

IT is the nature of compassion to associate with misfortune; and I address this to you in behalf even of an enemy, a captain in the British service, now on his way to the head-quarters of the American army, and unfortunately doomed to death for a crime not his own. A sentence so extraordinary, an execution so repugnant to every human sensation, ought never to be told without the circumstances which produced it; and as the destined victim is yet in existence, and in your hands rest his life or death, I shall briefly state the case, and the melancholy consequence.

Captain Hudd, of the Jersey militia, was attacked in a small fort on Tom's River, by a party of refugees in the British pay and service, was made prisoner, together with his company, carried to New York and lodged in the provost of that city: about three weeks after which, he was taken out of the provost down to the water-side, put into a boat, and brought again upon the Jersey shore; and there, contrary to the practice of all nations but savages, was hung up on a tree, and left hanging till found by our people, who took him down and buried him.

The inhabitants of that part of the country where the murder was committed, sent a deputation to General Washington, with a full and certified statement of the fact. Struck, as every human breast must be, with such brutish outrage, and determined both to punish and prevent it for the future, the general represented the case to General Clinton, who then commanded, and demanded that the refugee officer who ordered and attended the execution, and whose name is Lippincut, should be delivered up as a murderer; and in case of refusal, that the person of some British officer should suffer in his stead. The demand, though not refused, has not been complied with; and the melancholy lot (not by selection, but by casting lots) has fallen upon Captain Asgill, of the guards, who, as I have already mentioned, is on his way from Lancaster to camp, a martyr to the general wickedness of the cause he engaged in, and the ingratitude of those whom he served.

The first reflection which arises on this black business is, what sort of men must Englishmen be, and what sort of order and discipline do they preserve in their army, when in the immediate place of their head quarters, and under the eye and nose of their commander-in-chief, a prisoner can be taken at pleasure from his confinement, and his death made a matter of sport?

The history of the most savage Indians does not produce instances exactly of this kind. They, at least, have a formality in their punishments. With them it is the horridness of revenge, but with your army it is a still greater crime, the horridness of diversion.

The British generals who have succeeded each other, from the time of General Gage to yourself, have all affected to speak in language that they have no right to. In their proclamations, their addresses, their letters to General Washington, and their supplications to Congress (for they deserve no other name) they talk of British honor, British generosity, and British clemency, as if those things were matters of fact; whereas, we whose eyes are open, who speak the same language with yourselves, many of whom were born on the same spot with you, and who can no more be mistaken in your words than in your actions, can declare to all the world, that so far as our knowledge goes, there is not a more detestable character, nor a meaner or more barbarous enemy, than the present British one. With us, you have forfeited all pretensions to reputation, and it is only holding you like a wild beast, afraid of your keepers, that you can be made manageable. But to return to the point in question.

Though I can think no man innocent who has lent his hand to destroy the country which he did not plant, and to ruin those that he could not enslave, yet, abstracted from all ideas of right and wrong on the original question, Captain Asgill, in the present case, is not the guilty man. The villain and the victim are here separated characters. You hold the one and we the other. You disown, or affect to disown and reprobate the conduct of Lippincut, yet you give him a sanctuary; and by so doing you as effectually become the executioner of Asgill, as if you had put the rope on his neck, and dismissed him from the world. Whatever your feelings on this extraordinary occasion may be, are best known to yourself. Within the grave of your own mind lies buried the fate of Asgill. He becomes the corpse of your will, or the survivor of your justice. Deliver up the one, and you save the other; withold the one, and the other dies by your choice.

On our part the case is exceedingly plain; *an officer has been taken from his confinement and murdered, and the murderer is within your lines.* Your army has been guilty of a thousand instances of equal cruelty, but they have been rendered equivocal, and sheltered from personal detection. Here the crime is fixed; and is one of those extraordinary cases which can neither be denied nor palliated, and to which the custom of war does not apply; for it never could be supposed that such a brutal outrage would ever be committed. It is an original in the history of civilized barbarians, and it is truly British.

On your part you are accountable to us for the personal

safety of the prisoners within your walls. Here can be no mistake; they can neither be spies nor suspected as such; your security is not endangered, nor your operations subjected to miscarriage, by men immured within a dungeon. They differ in every circumstance from men in the field, and leave no pretence for severity of punishment. But if to the dismal condition of captivity with you, must be added the constant apprehension of death; if to be imprisoned is so nearly to be entombed; and, if after all, the murderers are to be protected, and thereby the crime encouraged, wherein do you differ from Indians, either in conduct or character?

We can have no idea of your honor or your justice, in any future transaction, of whatever nature it may be, while you shelter within your lines an outrageous murderer, and sacrifice in his stead an officer of your own. If you have no regard to us, at least spare the blood which it is your duty to save. Whether the punishment will be greater on him, who, in this case, innocently dies, or on him whom sad necessity forces to retaliate, is, in the nicety of sensation, an undecided question? It rests with you to prevent the sufferings of both. You have nothing to do but to give up the murderer, and the matter ends.

But to protect him, be he who he may, is to patronize his crime, and to trifle it off by frivolous and unmeaning inquiries, is to promote it. There is no declaration you can make nor promise you can give, that will obtain credit. It is the man and not the apology that is demanded.

You see yourself pressed on all sides to spare the life of your own officer, for die he will if you withold justice. The murder of Captain Huddy is an offence not to be borne with, and there is no security we can have that such actions or similar ones shall not be repeated, but by making the punishment fall upon yourselves. To destroy the last security of captivity, and to take the unarmed, the unresisting prisoner to private and sportive execution, is carrying barbarity too high for silence. The evil *must* be put an end to; and the choice of persons rests with you. But if your attachment to the guilty is stronger than to the innocent, you invent a crime that must destroy your character, and if the cause of your king needs to be so supported, for ever cease, sir, to torture our remembrance with the wretched phrases of British honor, British generosity, and British clemency.

From this melancholy circumstance, learn, sir, a lesson of morality. The refugees are men whom your predecessors have instructed in wickedness, the better to fit them to their master's purpose. To make them useful, they have made them vile, and the consequence of their tutored villainy is now descending on the heads of their encouragers. They have been trained like hounds to the scent of blood, and cherished in every species of dissolute barbarity. Their ideas of right and wrong are worn away in the constant habitude of repeated infamy, till, like men practised in executions, they feel not the value of another's life.

The task before you, though painful, is not difficult; give up the murderer, and save your officer, as the first outset of a necessary reformation.

COMMON SENSE.
Philadelphia, May 31, 1782.

THE CRISIS
NUMBER XIV

To the Earl of Shelburne

MY LORD,—A speech, which has been printed in several of the British and New York newspapers as coming from your lordship, in answer to one from the Duke of Richmond of the 10th of July last, contains expressions and opinions so new and singular, and so enveloped in mysterious reasoning, that I address this publication to you, for the purpose of giving them a free and candid examination. The speech that I allude to is in these words:

"His lordship said, it had been mentioned in another place, that he had been guilty of inconsistency. To clear himself of this, he asserted that he still held the same principles in respect to American independence which he at first imbibed. He had been, and yet was of opinion, whenever the parliament of Great Britain acknowledges that point, the sun of England's glory is set forever. Such were the sentiments he possessed on a former day, and such the sentiments he continued to hold at this hour. It was the opinion of Lord Chatham, as well as many other able statesmen. Other noble lords however, think differently; and as the majority of the cabinet support them, he acquiesced in the measure, dissenting from the idea; and the point is settled for bringing the matter into the full discussion of parliament, where it will be candidly, fairly, and impartially debated. The independence of America would end in the ruin of England; and that a peace patched up with France, would give that proud enemy the means of yet trampling on this country. The sun of England's glory he wished not to see set forever; he looked for a spark at least to be left, which might in time light us up to a new day. But if independence was to be granted, if parliament deemed that measure prudent, he forsaw, in his own mind, that England was undone. He wished to God that he had been deputed to Congress, that he might plead the cause of that country as well as of this, and that he might exercise whatever powers he possessed as an orator, to save both from ruin, by striving to convince Congress that, if their independence was signed, their liberties were gone forever.

"Peace, his lordship added, was a desirable object, but it must be an honorable peace, and not a humiliating one, dictated by France or insisted on by America. It was very true, that this kingdom was not in a flourishing state; it was impoverished by war. But if we were not rich, it was evident that France was poor. If we were straitened in our finances, the enemy were exhausted in their resources. This was a great empire; it abounded with brave men, who were able and willing to fight in a common cause; the language of humiliation should not, therefore, be the language of Great Britain. His lordship said, that he was not afraid nor ashamed of those expressions going to America. There were numbers, great numbers there, who were of the same way of thinking in respect to that country being dependent on this, and who, with his lordship, perceived ruin and independence linked together."

Thus far the speech; on which I remark—That his lordship is a total stranger to the mind and sentiments of America; that he has wrapped himself up in a fond delusion, that something less than independence may, under his administration, be accepted; and he wishes himself sent to Congress, to prove the most extraordinary of all doctrines, which is, that *independence*, the sublimest of all human conditions, is loss of liberty.

In answer to which we may say, that in order to know what the contrary word *dependance* means, we have only to look back to those years of severe humiliation, when the mildest of all petitions could obtain no other notice than the haughtiest of all insults; and when the base terms of unconditional submission were demanded, or undistinguishable destruction threatened. It is nothing to us that the ministry have been changed, for they may be changed again. The guilt of a government is the crime of a whole country; and the nation that can, though but for a moment, think and act as England has done, can never afterwards be believed or trusted. There are cases in which it is as impossible to restore character to life, as it is to recover the dead. It is a phoenix that can expire but once, and from whose ashes there is no resurrection. Some offences are of such a slight composition, that they reach no further than the temper, and are created or cured by a thought. But the sin of England has struck the heart of America, and nature has not left it in our power to say we can forgive.

Your lordship wishes for an opportunity to plead before Congress *the cause of England and America, and to save*, as you say, *both from ruin*.

That the country, which for more than seven years has sought our destruction, should now cringe to solicit our protection, is adding the wretchedness of disgrace to the misery of disappointment; and if England has the least spark of supposed honor left, that spark must be darkened by asking, and extinguished by receiving, the smallest favor from America; for the criminal who owes his life to the grace and mercy of the injured, is more executed by living than he who dies.

But a thousand pleadings, even from your lordship, can

have no effect. Honor, interest, and every sensation of the heart, would plead against you. We are a people who think not as you think; and what is equally true, you cannot feel as we feel. The situations of the two countries are exceedingly different. Ours has been the seat of war; yours has seen nothing of it. The most wanton destruction has been committed in our sight; the most insolent barbarity has been acted on our feelings. We can look round and see the remains of burnt and destroyed houses, once the fair fruit of hard industry, and now the striking monuments of British brutality. We walk over the dead whom we loved, in every part of America, and remember by whom they fell. There is scarcely a village but brings to life some melancholy thought, and reminds us of what we have suffered, and of those we have lost by the inhumanity of Britain. A thousand images arise to us, which, from situation, you cannot see, and are accompanied by as many ideas which you cannot know; and therefore your supposed system of reasoning would apply to nothing, and all your expectations die of themselves.

The question whether England shall accede to the independence of America, and which your lordship says is to undergo a parliamentary discussion, is so very simple, and composed of so few cases, that it scarcely needs a debate.

It is the only way out of an expensive and ruinous war, which has no object, and without which acknowledgment there can be no peace.

But your lordship says, *"the sun of Great Britain will set whenever she acknowledges the independence of America."*— Whereas the metaphor would have been strictly just, to have left the sun wholly out of the figure, and have ascribed her not acknowledging it to the influence of the moon.

But the expression, if true, is the greatest confession of disgrace that could be made, and furnishes America with the highest notions of sovereign independent importance. Mr. Wedderburne, about the year 1776, made use of an idea of much the same kind,—*"Relinquish America!"* says he—*"What is it but to desire a giant to shrink spontaneously into a dwarf"*

Alas! are those people, who call themselves Englishmen, of so little internal consequence, that when America is gone or shuts her eyes upon them, their sun is set, they can shine no more, but grope about in obscurity, and contract into insignificant animals? Was America, then, the giant of the empire, and England only her dwarf in waiting? Is the case so strangely altered, that those who once thought we could not live without them, are now brought to declare that they cannot exist without us? Will they tell to the world, and that from their first minister of state, that America is their all in all; that it is by her importance only they can live, and breathe, and have a being? Will they, who long since threatened to bring us to their feet, bow themselves at ours, and own that without us they are not a nation? Are they become so unqualified to debate on independence, that they have lost all idea of it themselves, and are calling to the rocks and mountains of America to cover their insignificance? Or, if America is lost, is it manly to sob over it like a child for its rattle, and invite the laughter of the world by declarations of disgrace? Surely, the more consistent conduct would be to bear it without complaint; and to show that England, without America, can preserve her independence, and a suitable rank with other European powers. You were not contented while you had her, and to weep for her now is childish.

But Lord Shelburne thinks something may yet be done. What that something is, or how it is to be accomplished, is a matter in obscurity. By arms there is no hope. The experience of nearly eight years, with the expense of 100,000,000 pounds sterling, and the loss of two armies, must positively decide that point. Besides, the British have lost their interest in America with the disaffected. Every part of it has been tried. There is no new scene left for delusion: and the thousands who have been ruined by adhering to them, and have now to quit the settlements they had acquired, and be conveyed like transports to cultivate the deserts of Augustine and Nova Scotia, has put an end to all further expectations of aid.

If you cast your eyes on the people of England, what have they to console themselves with for the millions expended? Or what encouragement is there left to continue throwing good money after bad? America can carry on the war for ten years longer, and all the charges of government included, for less than you can defray the charges of war and government for one year. And I, who know both countries, know well, that the people of America can afford to pay their share of the expense much better than the people of England can. Besides, it is their own estates and property, their own rights, liberties and government, they are defending; and were they not to do it, they would deserve to lose all, and none would pity them. The fault would be their own, and their punishment just.

The British army in America care not how long the war lasts. They enjoy an easy and indolent life. They fatten on the folly of one country and the spoils of another; and, between their plunder and their pay, may go home rich. But the case is very different with the laboring farmer, the working tradesman, and the necessitous poor in England, the sweat of whose brow goes day after day to feed, in prodigality and sloth, the army that is robbing both them and us. Removed from the eye of the country that supports them, and distant from the government that employs them, they cut and carve for themselves, and there is none to call them to account.

But England will be ruined, says Lord Shelburne, if America is independent.

Then, I say, is England already ruined, for America is already independent: and if Lord Shelburne will not allow this, he immediately denies the fact which he infers. Besides, to make England the mere creature of America, is paying too great a compliment to us, and too little to himself.

But the declaration is a rhapsody of inconsistency. For to say, as Lord Shelburne has numberless times said, that the war against America is ruinous, and yet to continue the prosecution of that ruinous war for the purpose of avoiding ruin, is a language which cannot be understood. Neither is it possible to see how the independence of America is to accomplish the ruin of England after the war is over, and yet not affect it before. America cannot be more independent of her, nor a greater enemy to her, hereafter than she now is; nor can England derive less advantages from her than at present. Why then is ruin to follow in the best state of the case, and not in the worst? And if not in the worst, why is it to follow at all?

That a nation is to be ruined by peace and commerce, and fourteen or fifteen millions a year less expenses than before, is a new doctrine in politics. We have heard much clamor of national savings and economy; but surely the true economy would be, to save the whole charge of a silly, foolish, and headstrong war; because, compared with this, all other retrenchments are baubles and trifles.

But is it possible that Lord Shelburne can be serious in supposing the least advantage can be obtained by arms, or that any advantage can be equal to the expense or the danger of attempting it? Will not the capture of one army after another satisfy him; must all become prisoners? Must England ever be the sport of hope and the victim of delusion? Sometimes, our currency was to fail; another time, our army was to disband: then, whole provinces were to revolt. Such a general said this and that; another wrote so and so; Lord Chatham was of this opinion; and Lord somebody else of another. To-day, 20,000 Russians and 20 Russian ships of the line were to come; to-morrow, the empress was abused without mercy or decency. Then the emperor of Germany was to be bribed with a million of money, and the king of Prussia was to do wonderful things. At one time it was, Lo here! and then it was, Lo there! Some-times this power, and sometimes that power, was to engage in the war, just, as if the whole world was as mad and foolish as Britain. And thus, from year to year, has every straw been catched at, and every Will-with-a-wisp led them a new dance.

This year a still newer folly is to take place. Lord Shel-burne wishes to be sent to Congress, and he thinks that some-thing may be done.

Are not the repeated declarations of Congress, and which all America supports, that they will not even hear any pro-posals whatever, until the unconditional and unequivocal inde-pendence of America is recognized; are not, I say, these decla-rations answer enough?

But for England to receive anything from America now, after so many insults, injuries and outrages acted towards us, would show such a spirit of meanness in her, that we could not but despise her for accepting it. And so far from Lord Shel-burne coming here to solicit it, it would be the greatest dis-grace we could do them to offer it. England would appear a wretch indeed, at this time of day, to ask or owe anything to the bounty of America. Has not the name of Englishman blots enough upon it, without inventing more? Even Lucifer would scorn to reign in heaven by permission, and yet an Englishman can creep for only an entrance into America. Or, has a land of liberty so many charms, that to be a door-keeper in it is better than to be an English minister of state?

But what can this expected something be? Or, if obtained, what can it amount to, but new disgraces, contentions and quarrels? The people of America have for years accustomed themselves to think and speak so freely and contemptuously of English authority, and the inveteracy is so deeply rooted, that a person invested with any authority from that country, and attempting to exercise it here, would have the life of a toad under a harrow. They would look upon him as an interloper, to whom their compassion permitted a residence. He would be no more than the Mungo of a farce; and if he disliked that, he must set off. It would be a station of degradation, debased by our pity, and despised by our pride, and would place England in a more contemptible situation than any she has yet suffered by the war. We have too high an opinion of ourselves, ever to think of yielding again the least obedience to outlandish authority; and for a thousand reasons, England would be the last country in the world to yield it to. She has been treacherous, and we know it. Her character is gone, and we have seen the funeral.

Surely she loves to fish in troubled waters, and drink the cup of contention, or she would not now think of mingling her affairs with those of America. It would be like a foolish dotard taking to his arms the bride that despises him, or who has placed on his head the ensigns of her disgust. It is kissing the hand that boxes his ears, and proposing to renew the exchange. The thought is as servile as the war is wicked, and shows the last scene of the drama as inconsistent as the first.

As America is gone, the only act of manhood is to *let her go*. Your lordship had no hand in the separation, and you will gain no honor by temporizing politics. Besides, there is something so exceedingly whimsical, unsteady, and even insincere in the present conduct of England, that she exhibits herself in the most dishonorable colors.

On the 2nd of August last General Carlton and Admiral Digby wrote to General Washington in these words:

"The resolution of the House of Commons of the 27th of February last, has been placed in your excellency's hands, and intimations given at the same time that further pacific measures were likely to follow. Since which, until the present time, we have had no direct communications from England; but a mail is now arrived, which brings us very important information. We are acquainted, sir, *by authority*, that negotiations for a general peace have already commenced at Paris, and that Mr. Grenville is invested with full powers to treat with all the parties at war, and is now at Paris in the execution of his commission. And we are further, sir, made acquainted, *that his majesty, in order to remove any obstacles to that peace which he so ardently wishes to restore, has commanded his ministers to direct Mr. Grenville, that the independence of the Thirteen United Provinces, should be proposed by him in the first instance, instead of making it a condition of a general treaty.*"

Now, taking your present measures into view, and comparing them with the declaration in this letter, pray, what is the word of your king, or his ministers, or the parliament good for? Must we not look upon you as a confederated body of faithless, treacherous men, whose assurances are fraud, and their language deceit? What opinion can we possibly form of you, but that you are a lost, abandoned, profligate nation, who sport even with your own character, and are to be held by nothing but the bayonet or the halter?

To say, after this, *that the sun of Great Britain will be set whenever she acknowledges the independence of America,* when the not doing it is the unqualified lie of government, can be no other than the language of ridicule, the jargon of inconsistency. There were thousands in America who predicted the delusion, and looked upon it as a trick of treachery, to take us from our guard, and draw off our attention from the only system of finance, by which we can be called, or deserve to be called, a sovereign, independent people. The fraud, on your part, might be worth attempting, but the sacrifice to obtain it is too high.

There are others who credited the assurance, because they thought it impossible that men who had their characters to establish, would begin it with a lie. The prosecution of the war by the former ministry was savage and horrid; since which it has been mean, trickish, and delusive. The one went greedily into the passion of revenge, the other into the subtleties of low contrivance; till, between the crimes of both, there is scarcely left a man in America, be he whig or tory, who does not despise or detest the conduct of Britain.

The management of Lord Shelburne, whatever may be his views, is a caution to us, and must be to the world, never to regard British assurances. A perfidy so notorious cannot be hid. It stands even in the public papers of New York, with the names of Canton and Digby affixed to it. It is a proclamation that the king of England is not to be believed: that the spirit of lying is the governing principle of the ministry. It is holding up the character of the House of Commons to public infamy, and warning all men not to credit them. Such are the consequences which Lord Shelburne's management has brought upon his country.

After the authorized declarations contained in Canton and Digby's letter, you ought, from every motive of honor, policy, and prudence, to have fulfilled them, whatever might have been the event. It was the least atonement you could possibly make to America, and the greatest kindness you could do to yourselves; for you will save millions by a general peace and you will lose as many by continuing the war.

COMMON SENSE.
Philadelphia, October 29, 1782.

P. S.—The manuscript copy of this letter is sent your lordship, by the way of our head-quarters, to New York, inclosing a late pamphlet of mine, addressed to the Abbé Raynal, which will serve to give your lordship some idea of the principles and sentiments of America. C. S.

THE CRISIS
NUMBER XV

"THE times that tried men's souls,"* are over—and the greatest and completest revolution the world ever knew, is gloriously and happily accomplished.

But to pass from the extremes of danger to safety—from the tumult of war to the tranquillity of peace, though sweet in contemplation, requires a gradual composure of the senses to receive it. Even calmness has the power of stunning, when it opens too instantly upon us. The long and raging hurricane that should cease in a moment, would leave us in a state rather of wonder than enjoyment; and some moments of recollection must pass, before we could be capable of tasting the felecity of repose. There are but few instances, in which the mind is fitted for sudden transitions: it takes in its pleasures by reflection and comparison, and those must have time to act, before the relish for new scenes is complete.

In the present case—the mighty magnitude of the object—the various uncertainties of fate it has undergone— the numerous and complicated dangers we have suffered or escaped—the eminence we now stand on, and the vast prospect before us, must all conspire to impress us with contemplation.

To see it in our power to make a world happy—to teach mankind the art of being so—to exhibit, on the theatre of the universe, a character hitherto unknown —and to have, as it were, a new creation intrusted to our hands, are honors that

---

* "These are the times that try men's souls." *The Crisis* No.1, published December, 1776.

command reflection, and can neither be too highly estimated, nor too gratefully received.

In this pause then of recollection—while the storm is ceasing, and the long agitated mind vibrating to a rest, let us look back on the scenes we have passed, and learn from experience what is yet to be done.

Never, I say, had a country so many openings to happiness as this. Her setting out in life, like the rising of a fair morning, was unclouded and promising. Her cause was good. Her principles just and liberal. Her temper serene and firm. Her conduct regulated by the nicest steps, and every thing about her wore the mark of honor. It is not every country (perhaps there is not another in the world) that can boast so fair an origin. Even the first settlement of America corresponds with the character of the revolution. Rome, once the proud mistress of the universe, was originally a band of ruffians. Plunder and rapine made her rich, and her oppression of millions made her great. But America need never be ashamed to tell her birth, nor relate the stages by which she rose to empire.

The remembrance, then, of what is past, if it operates rightly, must inspire her with the most laudable of all ambition, that of adding to the fair fame she began with. The world has seen her great in adversity. Struggling, without a thought of yielding, beneath accumulated difficulties. Bravely, nay proudly, encountering distress, and rising in resolution as the storm increased. All this is justly due to her, for her fortitude has merited the character. Let, then, the world see that she can bear prosperity; and that her honest virtue in time of peace, is equal to the bravest virtue in time of war.

She is now descending to the scenes of quiet and domestic life. Not beneath the cypress shade of disappointment, but to enjoy in her own land, and under her own vine, the sweet of her labors, and the reward of her toil.—In this situation, may she never forget that a fair national reputation is of as much importance as independence. That it possesses a charm that wins upon the world, and makes even enemies civil.—That it gives a dignity which is often superior to power, and commands reverence where pomp and splendor fail.

It would be a circumstance ever to be lamented and never to be forgotten, were a single blot, from any cause whatever, suffered to fall on a revolution, which to the end of time must be an honor to the age that accomplished it: and which has contributed more to enlighten the world, and diffuse a spirit of freedom and liberality among mankind, than any human event (if this may be called one) that ever preceded it.

It is not among the least of the calamities of a long continued war, that it unhinges the mind from those nice sensations which at other times appear so amiable. The continual spectacle of woe blunts the finer feelings, and the necessity of bearing with the sight, renders it familiar. In like manner, are many of the moral obligations of society weakened, till the custom of acting by necessity becomes an apology, where it is truly a crime. Yet let but a nation conceive rightly of its character, and it will be chastely just in protecting it. None ever began with a fairer than America, and none can be under a greater obligation to preserve it.

The debt which America has contracted, compared with the cause she has gained, and the advantages to flow from it, ought scarcely to be mentioned. She has it in her choice to do, and to live as happily as she pleases. The world is in her hands. She has no foreign power to monopolize her commerce, perplex her legislation, or control her prosperity. The struggle is over, which must one day have happened, and, perhaps, never could have happened at a better time.* And instead of a domineering master, she has gained an *ally*, whose exemplary greatness, and universal liberality, have extorted a confession even from her enemies.

With the blessings of peace, independence, and an universal commerce, the states, individually and collectively, will have leisure and opportunity to regulate and establish their domestic concerns, and to put it beyond the power of calumny to throw the least reflection on their honor. Character is much easier kept than recovered, and that man, if any such there be,

---

*That the revolution began at the exact period of time best fitted to the purpose, is sufficiently proved by the event.—But the great hinge on which the whole machine turned, is the *Union of the States*: and this union was naturally produced by the inability of any one state to support itself against any foreign enemy without the assistance of the rest.

Had the states severally been less able than they were when the war began, their united strength would not have been equal to the undertaking, and they must in all human probability have failed.—And, on the other hand, had they severally been more able, they might not have seen, or, what is more, might not have felt, the necessity of uniting: and, either by attempting to stand alone or in small confederacies, would have been separately conquered.

Now, as we cannot see a time (and many years must pass away before it can arrive) when the strength of any one state, or several united, can be equal to the whole of the present United States, and as we have seen the extreme difficulty of collectively prosecuting the war to a successful issue, and preserving our national Importance in the world, therefore, from the experience we have had, and the knowledge we have gained, we must, unless we make a waste of wisdom, be strongly impressed with the advantage, as well as the necessity of strengthening that happy union which has been our salvation, and without which we should have been a ruined people.

While I was writing this note, I cast my eye on the pamphlet, *Common Sense*, from which I shall make an extract, as it applies exactly to the case. It is as follows:

"I have never met with a man, either in England or America, who hath not confessed it as his opinion that a separation between the countries would take place one time or other; and there is no instance in which we have shown less judgment, than in endeavoring to describe, what we call, the ripeness or fitness of the continent for independence.

"As all men allow the measure, and differ only in their opinion of the time, let us, in order to remove mistakes, take a general survey of things, and endeavor, if possible, to find out the *very time*. But we need not to go far, the inquiry ceases at once, for, *the time hath found us*. The general concurrence, the glorious union of all things prove the fact.

"It is not in numbers, but in a union, that our great strength lies. The continent is just arrived at that pitch of strength, in which no single colony is able to support itself, and the whole, when united, can accomplish the matter; and either more or less than this, might be fatal in its effects."

who, from sinister views, or littleness of soul, lends unseen his hand to injure it, contrives a wound it will never be in his power to heal.

As we have established an inheritance for posterity, let that inheritance descend, with every mark of an honorable conveyance. The little it will cost, compared with the worth of the states, the greatness of the object, and the value of national character, will be a profitable exchange.

But that which must more forcibly strike a thoughtful, penetrating mind, and which includes and renders easy all inferior concerns, is the *Union of the States*. On this our great national character depends. It is this which must give us importance abroad and security at home. It is through this only, that we are, or can be nationally known in the world; it is the flag of the United States which renders our ships and commerce safe on the seas, or in a foreign port. Our Mediterranean passes must be obtained under the same style. All our treaties, whetherof alliance, peace or commerce, are formed under the sovereignty of the United States, and Europe knows us by no other name or title.

The division of the empire into states is for our own convenience, but abroad this distinction ceases. The affairs of each state are local. They can go no further than to itself. And were the whole worth of even the richest of them expended in revenue, it would not be sufficient to support sovereignty against a foreign attack. In short, we have no other national sovereignty than as United States. It would even be fatal for us if we had—too expensive to be maintained, and impossible to be supported. Individuals, or individual states, may call themselves what they please; but the world, and especially the world of enemies, is not to be held in awe by the whistling of a name. Sovereignty must have power to protect all the parts that compose and constitute it: and as UNITED STATES we are equal to the importance of the title, but otherwise we are not. Our union, well and wisely regulated and cemented, is the cheapest way of being great—the easiest way of being powerful, and the happiest invention in government which the circumstances of America can admit of.—Because it collects from each state, that which, by being inadequate, can be of no use to it, and forms an aggregate that serves for all.

The states of Holland are an unfortunate instance of the effects of individual sovereignty. Their disjointed condition exposes them to numerous intrigues, losses, calamities and enemies; and the almost impossibility of bringing their measures to a decision, and that decision into execution, is to them, and would be to us, a source of endless misfortune.

It is with confederated states as with individuals in society; something must be yielded up to make the whole secure. In this view of things we gain by what we give, and draw an annual interest greater than the capital. I ever feel myself hurt when I hear the union, the great palladium of our liberty and safety, the least irreverently spoken of. It is the most sacred thing in the constitution of America, and that which every man should be most proud and tender of. Our citizenship in the United States is our national character. Our citizenship in any particular state is only our local distinction. By the latter we are known at home, by the former to the world. Our great title is AMERICANS—our inferior one varies with the place.

So far as my endeavors could go, they have all been directed to conciliate the affections, unite the interests, and draw and keep the mind of the country together; and the better to assist in this foundation work of the revolution, I have avoided all places of profit or office, either in the state I live in, or in the United States; kept myself at a distance from all parties and party connections, and even disregarded all private and inferior concerns: and when we take into view the great work which we have gone through, and feel, as we ought to feel, the just importance of it, we shall then see, that the little wranglings and indecent contentions of personal parley, are as dishonorable to our characters, as they are injurious to our repose.

It was the cause of America that made me an author. The force with which it struck my mind, and the dangerous condition the country appeared to me in, by courting an impossible and an unnatural reconciliation with those who were determined to reduce her, instead of striking out into the only line that could cement and save her,—a DECLARATION OF INDEPENDENCE,—made it impossible for me, feeling as I did, to be silent: and if, in the course of more than seven years, I have rendered her any service, I have likewise added something to the reputation of literature by freely and disinterestedly employing it in the great cause of mankind, and showing that there may be genius without prostitution.

Independence always appeared to me practicable and probable; provided the sentiment of the country could be formed and held to the object: and there is no instance in the world, where a people so extended, and wedded to former habits of thinking, and under such a variety of circumstances, were so instantly and effectually pervaded, by a turn in politics, as in the case of independence, and who supported their opinion, undiminished, through such a succession of good and ill fortune, till they crowned it with success.

But as the scenes of war are closed, and every man preparing for home and happier times, I therefore take my leave of the subject. I have most sincerely followed it from beginning to end, and through all its turns and windings: and whatever country I may hereafter be in, I shall always feel an honest pride at the part I have taken and acted, and a gratitude to Nature and Providence for putting it in my power to be of some use to mankind.

COMMON SENSE.
Philadelphia, April 19, 1783.

THE CRISIS
NUMBER XVI

To the People of America

IN *"Rivington's New York Gazette,"* of December 6th, is a
publication, under the appearance of a letter from London,
dated Sept. 30th; and is on a subject which demands the
attention of the United States.

The public will remember, that a treaty of commerce
between the United States and England was set on foot last
spring, and that until the said treaty could be completed, a bill
was brought into the British Parliament, by the then chancellor
of the exchequer, Mr. Pitt, to admit and legalize (as the case
then required) the commerce of the United States into the
British ports and dominions. But neither the one nor the other
has been completed. The commercial treaty is broken off, or
remains as it began; and the bill in parliament has been thrown
aside. And in lieu thereof, a selfish system of English politics
has started up, calculated to fetter the commerce of America,
by engrossing to England the carrying trade of the American
produce to the West India Islands.

Among the advocates for this last measure is Lord
Sheffield, a member of the British Parliament, who has published a pamphlet entitled, *"Observations on the Commerce of
the American States."* The pamphlet has two objects; the one
is, to allure the Americans to purchase British manufactures;
and the other, to spirit up the British Parliament to prohibit the
citizens of the United States from trading to the West India
Islands.

Viewed in this light, the pamphlet, though in some parts dexterously written, is an absurdity. It offends, in the very act of endeavoring to ingratiate; and his lordship, as a politician, ought not to have suffered the two objects to have appeared together. The letter alluded to contains extracts from the pamphlet, with high encomiums on Lord Sheffield, for laboriously endeavoring (as the letter styles it) "to show the mighty advantages of retaining the carrying trade."

Since the publication of this pamphlet in England, the commerce of the United States to the West Indies in American vessels, has been prohibited; and all intercourse, except in British bottoms, (the property of, and navigated by British subjects), cut off.

That a country has a right to be as foolish as it pleases, has been proved by the practice of England for many years past. In her island situation, sequestered from the world, she forgets that her whispers are heard by other nations; and in her plans of politics and commerce, she seems not to know, that other votes are necessary besides her own. America would be equally as foolish as Britain, were she to suffer so great a degradation on her flag, and such a stroke on the freedom of her commerce, to pass without a balance.

We admit the right of any nation to prohibit the commerce of another into its own dominions, where there are no treaties to the contrary; but as this right belongs to one side, as well as the other, there is always a way left to bring avarice and insolence to reason.

But the ground of security which Lord Sheffield has chosen to erect his policy upon, is of a nature which ought, and I think must awaken, in every American, a just and strong sense of national dignity. Lord Sheffield appears to be sensible, that in advising the British nation and parliament to engross to themselves so great a part of the carrying trade of America, he is attempting a measure which cannot succeed, if the politics of the United States be properly directed to counteract the assumption. But, says he, in his pamphlet, *"It will be a long time before the American States can be brought to act as a nation, neither are they to be feared as such by us."*

What is this more or less than to tell us, that while we have no national system of commerce, the British will govern our trade by their own laws and proclamations as they please. The quotation discloses a truth too serious to be overlooked, and too mischievous not to be remedied.

Among other circumstances which led them to this discovery, none could operate so effectually, as the injudicious, uncandid and indecent opposition made by sundry persons in a certain state, to the recommendations of Congress last winter, for an import duty of five per cent. It could not but explain to the British a weakness in the national power of America, and encourage them to attempt restrictions on her trade, which otherwise they would not have dared to hazard. Neither is there any state in the union, whose policy was more misdirected to its interest than the state I allude to, because her principal support is the carrying trade, which Britain, induced by the want of a well-centered power in the United States to protect and secure, is now attempting to take away. It fortunately happened (and to no state in the union more than the state in question) that the terms of peace were agreed on before the opposition appeared, otherwise, there needs not a doubt, that if the same idea of the diminished authority of America had occurred to them at that time as has occurred to them since, but they would have made the same grasp at the fisheries, as they have done at the carrying trade.

It is surprising that an authority which can be supported

with so much ease, and so little expense, and capable of such extensive advantages to the country, should be cavilled at by those whose duty it is to watch over it, and whose existence as a people depends upon it. But this, perhaps, will ever be the case, till some misfortune awakens us into reason, and the instance now before us is but a gentle beginning of what America must expect, unless she guards her union with nicer care and stricter honor. United, she is formidable, and that with the least possible charge a nation can be so. Separated, she is a medley of individual nothings, subject to the sport of foreign nations.

It is very probable that the ingenuity of commerce may have found out a method to evade and supersede the intentions of the British, in interdicting the trade with the West India Islands. The language of both being the same, and their customs well understood, the vessels of one country may, by deception, pass for those of another. But this would be a practice too debasing for a sovereign people to stoop to, and too profligate not to be discountenanced. An illicit trade, under any shape it can be placed, cannot be carried on without a violation of truth. America is now sovereign and independent, and ought to act all her affairs in a regular style of character. She has the same right to say that no British vessel shall enter her port, or that no British manufactures shall be imported but in American bottoms, the property of, and navigated by American subjects, as Britain has to say the same thing respecting the West Indies. Or she may lay a duty of ten, fifteen or twenty shillings per ton (exclusive of other duties) on every British vessel coming from any port of the West Indies, where she is not admitted to trade, the said tonnage to continue as long on her side as the prohibition continues on the other.

But it is only by acting in union, that the usurpations of

foreign nations on the freedom of trade can be counteracted, and security extended to the commerce of America. And when we view a flag, which to the eye is beautiful, and to contemplate its rise and origin inspires a sensation of sublime delight, our national honor must unite with our interest to prevent injury to the one, or insult to the other.

COMMON SENSE.
New York, December 9, 1783.

GREAT MINDS PAPERBACK SERIES

ART

❑ Leonardo da Vinci—*A Treatise on Painting*

CRITICAL ESSAYS

❑ Desiderius Erasmus—*The Praise of Folly*
❑ Jonathan Swift—*A Modest Proposal and Other Satires*
❑ H. G. Wells—*The Conquest of Time*

ECONOMICS

❑ Charlotte Perkins Gilman—*Women and Economics: A Study of the Economic Relation between Women and Men*
❑ John Maynard Keynes—*The End of Laissez-Faire* and *The Economic Consequences of the Peace*
❑ John Maynard Keynes—*The General Theory of Employment, Interest, and Money*
❑ John Maynard Keynes—*A Tract on Monetary Reform*
❑ Thomas R. Malthus—*An Essay on the Principle of Population*
❑ Alfred Marshall—*Money, Credit, and Commerce*
❑ Alfred Marshall—*Principles of Economics*
❑ Karl Marx—*Theories of Surplus Value*
❑ John Stuart Mill—*Principles of Political Economy*
❑ David Ricardo—*Principles of Political Economy and Taxation*
❑ Adam Smith—*Wealth of Nations*
❑ Thorstein Veblen—*Theory of the Leisure Class*

HISTORY

❑ Edward Gibbon—*On Christianity*
❑ Alexander Hamilton, John Jay, and James Madison—*The Federalist*
❑ Herodotus—*The History*
❑ Thomas Paine—*The Crisis*
❑ Thucydides—*History of the Peloponnesian War*
❑ Andrew D. White—*A History of the Warfare of Science with Theology in Christendom*

LAW

❑ John Austin—*The Province of Jurisprudence Determined*

POLITICS

❑ Walter Lippmann—*A Preface to Politics*

PSYCHOLOGY

❑ Sigmund Freud—*Totem and Taboo*

RELIGION

❑ Thomas Henry Huxley—*Agnosticism and Christianity and Other Essays*
❑ Ernest Renan—*The Life of Jesus*
❑ Upton Sinclair—*The Profits of Religion*
❑ Elizabeth Cady Stanton—*The Woman's Bible*

❏ Voltaire—*A Treatise on Toleration and Other Essays*

SCIENCE

❏ Jacob Bronowski—*The Identity of Man*
❏ Nicolaus Copernicus—*On the Revolutions of Heavenly Spheres*
❏ Francis Crick—*Of Molecules and Men*
❏ Marie Curie—*Radioactive Substances*
❏ Charles Darwin—*The Autobiography of Charles Darwin*
❏ Charles Darwin—*The Descent of Man*
❏ Charles Darwin—*The Origin of Species*
❏ Charles Darwin—*The Voyage of the* Beagle
❏ René Descartes—*Treatise of Man*
❏ Albert Einstein—*Relativity*
❏ Michael Faraday—*The Forces of Matter*
❏ Galileo Galilei—*Dialogues Concerning Two New Sciences*
❏ Francis Galton—*Hereditary Genius*
❏ Ernst Haeckel—*The Riddle of the Universe*
❏ William Harvey—*On the Motion of the Heart and Blood in Animals*
❏ Werner Heisenberg—*Physics and Philosophy:
      The Revolution in Modern Science*
❏ Fred Hoyle—*Of Men and Galaxies*
❏ Julian Huxley—*Evolutionary Humanism*
❏ Thomas H. Huxley—*Evolution and Ethics* and *Science and Morals*
❏ Edward Jenner—*Vaccination against Smallpox*
❏ Johannes Kepler—*Epitome of Copernican Astronomy* and *Harmonies of the World*
❏ Charles Mackay—*Extraordinary Popular Delusions and the Madness of Crowds*
❏ James Clerk Maxwell—*Matter and Motion*
❏ Isaac Newton—*Opticks, Or Treatise of the Reflections, Inflections, and
      Colours of Light*
❏ Isaac Newton—*The Principia*
❏ Louis Pasteur and Joseph Lister—*Germ Theory and Its Application to Medicine* and *On
      the Antiseptic Principle of the Practice of Surgery*
❏ William Thomson (Lord Kelvin) and Peter Guthrie Tait—
      The Elements of Natural Philosophy
❏ Alfred Russel Wallace—*Island Life*

SOCIOLOGY

❏ Emile Durkheim—*Ethics and the Sociology of Morals*

GREAT BOOKS IN PHILOSOPHY PAPERBACK SERIES

ESTHETICS

❏ Aristotle—*The Poetics*
❏ Aristotle—*Treatise on Rhetoric*

ETHICS

❏ Aristotle—*The Nicomachean Ethics*
❏ Marcus Aurelius—*Meditations*
❏ Jeremy Bentham—*The Principles of Morals and Legislation*
❏ John Dewey—*Human Nature and Conduct*
❏ John Dewey—*The Moral Writings of John Dewey, Revised Edition*

❏ Epictetus—*Enchiridion*
❏ David Hume—*An Enquiry Concerning the Principles of Morals*
❏ Immanuel Kant—*Fundamental Principles of the Metaphysic of Morals*
❏ John Stuart Mill—*Utilitarianism*
❏ George Edward Moore—*Principia Ethica*
❏ Friedrich Nietzsche—*Beyond Good and Evil*
❏ Plato—*Protagoras, Philebus,* and *Gorgias*
❏ Bertrand Russell—*Bertrand Russell On Ethics, Sex, and Marriage*
❏ Arthur Schopenhauer—*The Wisdom of Life* and *Counsels and Maxims*
❏ Adam Smith—*The Theory of Moral Sentiments*
❏ Benedict de Spinoza—*Ethics* and *The Improvement of the Understanding*

LOGIC

❏ George Boole—*The Laws of Thought*

METAPHYSICS/EPISTEMOLOGY

❏ Aristotle—*De Anima*
❏ Aristotle—*The Metaphysics*
❏ Francis Bacon—*Essays*
❏ George Berkeley—*Three Dialogues Between Hylas and Philonous*
❏ W. K. Clifford—*The Ethics of Belief and Other Essays*
❏ René Descartes—*Discourse on Method* and *The Meditations*
❏ John Dewey—*How We Think*
❏ John Dewey—*The Influence of Darwin on Philosophy and Other Essays*
❏ Epicurus—*The Essential Epicurus: Letters, Principal Doctrines, Vatican Sayings, and Fragments*
❏ Sidney Hook—*The Quest for Being*
❏ David Hume—*An Enquiry Concerning Human Understanding*
❏ David Hume—*Treatise of Human Nature*
❏ William James—*The Meaning of Truth*
❏ William James—*Pragmatism*
❏ Immanuel Kant—*The Critique of Judgment*
❏ Immanuel Kant—*Critique of Practical Reason*
❏ Immanuel Kant—*Critique of Pure Reason*
❏ Gottfried Wilhelm Leibniz—*Discourse on Metaphysics* and the *Monadology*
❏ John Locke—*An Essay Concerning Human Understanding*
❏ George Herbert Mead—*The Philosophy of the Present*
❏ Michel de Montaigne—*Essays*
❏ Charles S. Peirce—*The Essential Writings*
❏ Plato—*The Euthyphro, Apology, Crito,* and *Phaedo*
❏ Plato—*Lysis, Phaedrus,* and *Symposium*
❏ Bertrand Russell—*The Problems of Philosophy*
❏ George Santayana—*The Life of Reason*
❏ Arthur Schopenhauer—*On the Principle of Sufficient Reason*
❏ Sextus Empiricus—*Outlines of Pyrrhonism*
❏ Ludwig Wittgenstein—*Wittgenstein's Lectures: Cambridge, 1932–1935*
❏ Alfred North Whitehead—*The Concept of Nature*

PHILOSOPHY OF RELIGION

❏ Jeremy Bentham—*The Influence of Natural Religion on the Temporal Happiness of Mankind*

❏ Marcus Tullius Cicero—*The Nature of the Gods* and *On Divination*
❏ Ludwig Feuerbach—*The Essence of Christianity* and *The Essence of Religion*
❏ Paul Henry Thiry, Baron d'Holbach—*Good Sense*
❏ David Hume—*Dialogues Concerning Natural Religion*
❏ William James—*The Varieties of Religious Experience*
❏ John Locke—*A Letter Concerning Toleration*
❏ Lucretius—*On the Nature of Things*
❏ John Stuart Mill—*Three Essays on Religion*
❏ Friedrich Nietzsche—*The Antichrist*
❏ Thomas Paine—*The Age of Reason*
❏ Bertrand Russell—*Bertrand Russell On God and Religion*

SOCIAL AND POLITICAL PHILOSOPHY

❏ Aristotle—*The Politics*
❏ Mikhail Bakunin—*The Basic Bakunin: Writings, 1869–1871*
❏ Jeremy Bentham—*The Rationale of Punishment*
❏ Edmund Burke—*Reflections on the Revolution in France*
❏ John Dewey—*Freedom and Culture*
❏ John Dewey—*Individualism Old and New*
❏ John Dewey—*Liberalism and Social Action*
❏ G. W. F. Hegel—*The Philosophy of History*
❏ G. W. F. Hegel—*Philosophy of Right*
❏ Thomas Hobbes—*The Leviathan*
❏ Sidney Hook—*Paradoxes of Freedom*
❏ Sidney Hook—*Reason, Social Myths, and Democracy*
❏ John Locke—*Second Treatise on Civil Government*
❏ Niccolo Machiavelli—*The Prince*
❏ Karl Marx (with Friedrich Engels)—*The German Ideology*, including
    Theses on Feuerbach and Introduction to the Critique of Political Economy
❏ Karl Marx—*The Poverty of Philosophy*
❏ Karl Marx/Friedrich Engels—*The Economic and Philosophic Manuscripts of 1844* and
    The Communist Manifesto
❏ John Stuart Mill—*Considerations on Representative Government*
❏ John Stuart Mill—*On Liberty*
❏ John Stuart Mill—*On Socialism*
❏ John Stuart Mill—*The Subjection of Women*
❏ Montesquieu, Charles de Secondat—*The Spirit of Laws*
❏ Friedrich Nietzsche—*Thus Spake Zarathustra*
❏ Thomas Paine—*Common Sense*
❏ Thomas Paine—*Rights of Man*
❏ Plato—*Laws*
❏ Plato—*The Republic*
❏ Jean-Jacques Rousseau—*Émile*
❏ Jean-Jacques Rousseau—*The Social Contract*
❏ Bertrand Russell—*Political Ideas*
❏ Mary Wollstonecraft—*A Vindication of the Rights of Men*
❏ Mary Wollstonecraft—*A Vindication of the Rights of Women*